THE REVOLUTIONARY NEW
PHYSICAL FITNESS PLAN!

Only after you've measured exercise in terms of essential benefits to your body will you understand why some of the most popular forms of exercise are almost worthless and why others, more neglected, score very high!

ASK YOUR PHYSICIAN ABOUT

AEROBICS

The only scientifically developed program of exercise—aimed at the overall fitness and health of your body—**that lets you measure your progress toward maximal health!**

QUANTITY PURCHASES

aerobics

by Kenneth H. Cooper, M.D., M.P.H.

BANTAM BOOKS
TORONTO • NEW YORK • LONDON • SYDNEY • AUCKLAND

AEROBICS

*A Bantam Book / published by arrangement with
M. Evans and Company, Inc.*

PRINTING HISTORY
Evans edition published April 1968
Portions of this book were excerpted in THIS WEEK *Magazine
March-April 1968 and in* READER'S DIGEST *March 1968*
Book-of-the-Month Club edition published Summer 1968

Bantam edition / April 1968
14 printings through March 1969
Revised Bantam edition / October 1969
31 printings through August 1980

CONTENTS

Dedication

To my Father,
who instilled in me an overwhelming
desire to study and practice the art
of preventive medicine, and
To my Mother,
who encouraged me in my athletic
endeavors during the formative years.

Acknowledgments

To complete a program of the type discussed in this
book required the cooperation of many people. I am
indebted to all for their assistance and particularly to
the "Poopers" who reached an unbelievable level of
fitness. I also want to thank the following people individually for their help and encouragement: Lt. Col.
Thurman Glasgow; Lt. Col. Robert Webb; Colonel
Clifford Raisor; and Dr. Arthur Grollman, University
of Texas. Particular thanks goes to Mr. Kevin Brown
for his extensive assistance in preparing the material.
Last but not least I want to especially thank my wife
for her constructive remarks, illimitable patience, and
hours and hours of manuscript typing.

DR. COOPER'S book should become a major contribution to a healthier America.

This is without question the best book on physical fitness that I have read. But it is much more than that.

Here is a highly readable, often amusing and always provocative book.

At the same time it contains the distillation of four years of intensive study by top medical experts on literally thousands of men to determine the relationship of physical fitness to health.

And Dr. Cooper has found it.

After all, what gift of the gods is more valuable than good health? All of us want it. All of us know we have to pay a price for it.

What most of us don't know is just what kind of price we have to pay. How much effort? How much pain if any? How much time? How much money?

This is what Dr. Cooper tells us. And the answer is surprisingly encouraging.

The money price is insignificant. The time price is very little indeed. The price in effort and pain? Well, there is a price. But believe me for most it will be eminently worthwhile.

This book will enable you to find out with a little pain and effort what your physical condition is right now.

It will tell you precisely how you can improve your condition. And it will give you a variety of alternative ways to exercise—to suit your temperament and inclination. The book will also tell you how to stay in condition.

I am convinced that if this book becomes a bestseller, and it certainly should; it will do more for the health and longevity of Americans than any other medical discovery or achievement of the year.

Death from heart disease is the number one killer in America today. Drugs, surgery, even transplants are making spectacular contributions to fighting this killer. But none of them can make as big and decisive a contribution to the battle for better health as this remarkable book by Dr. Cooper.

What is more, the book will not only save lives, it will make those lives more vital, alert, efficient and, yes, happy.

There's no doubt about the sheer euphoria that comes from following the Cooper prescription. There's also little question that your mind works more swiftly, and your stamina at work at a desk, in a conference, anywhere is improved by following the simple and—considering the benefits—the easy Cooper prescription.

INTRODUCTION

by Lt. General Richard L. Bohannon,
Surgeon General, United States Air Force (ret.)

PHYSICAL CONDITIONING and physical fitness have been given a great deal of attention by the American public in recent years. Many of our nation's leaders, notably the late President John F. Kennedy, have expressed their interest in and support of active physical fitness programs. The President's Council on Physical Fitness indicates continuing high-level interest in this important subject.

Interest has been stimulated by the realization that many of our people are not able to accomplish fairly simple physical fitness tests, and that most Americans, young and old, are devoting little time to activities requiring physical exertion. That regular physical exercise promotes the general health is generally acknowledged. Recently we have learned that regular, medically advised and supervised physical exercise is valuable in the rehabilitation of selected post-myocardial infarction patients, post-surgical patients, and patients who have been confined to bed for prolonged periods. We have also been stimulated to look to physical exercise as a possibly significant factor in reducing the incidence of heart disease and other chronic disorders, and in ameliorating the severity of certain other diseases. More research is required to delineate the exact role exercise can play.

The word "fitness," as applied to physical conditioning, has been an ill-defined, confusing term. For example, exactly where the ability to do forty push-ups or sixty sit-ups or twenty chinnings fits into the concept of general fitness is not well understood. To some people fitness connotes merely freedom from disease. Others measure fitness by the degree of muscular development present, by agility, or by proficiency in weight-lifting, gymnastics, skiing, or boxing. Still others include psychological well-being as an essential element. Fitness is a desirable state for anyone who wants to lead a zestful and productive life and realize his fullest potential. It deserves a concise definition. A high level of general fitness connotes freedom from disease, of course, and psychological well-being as well. But other components are also important. Reasonable muscular development, functional flexibility of the joints, adequate vital capacity of the lungs, reserve capacity of the heart and blood vessels, and stamina must all be included, with stamina in this context meaning the capacity to endure exertion and stressful physical activity as a reflection of good cardio-pulmonary reserve.

Much disability has been attributed to excessive inactivity. In this age of mechanization and automation, we know that our normal work activities do not provide the exercise which our bodies, our muscles, and our hearts and lungs require if they are to continue to function efficiently and effectively. Some investigators extend this thesis and deem the deconditioning phenomena resulting from inactivity to be a complex entity which might be called true hypokinetic disease.

Though not *all* is known about the body's need for exercise, nor about the appropriate kind and duration, Dr. Cooper's research makes a significant contribution by correlating oxygen consumption and pulse rate with various types of exercise and the vigor and duration of each. He has described a sort of pharmacopeia of exercise which gives us some idea of the training effect of each of several types of exercise and some concept of the value of each, as far as the building of the requisite cardio-pulmonary reserve is concerned. He differentiates between the so-called anaerobic and aerobic types of exercise, based on the oxygen consumption each requires, and quotes impressive figures to prove the greater effectiveness of the aerobic form. Admittedly, even aerobic exercise is not a panacea; but its essentiality in the building of good physical condition seems well documented. Longevity does not depend on the strength and tone of the muscles of the arms, legs, or abdominal wall. According to our present understanding of the matter, it is much more likely, in the absence of organic disease elsewhere, to depend on the capability of the cardio-vascular and pulmonary systems to withstand the stresses of modern living. Aerobic exercise, as described by Dr. Cooper, will assist the development of this capability. By regular participation, with his physician's approval, in an aerobic exercise program, coupled with weight control and the elimination of tobacco, an individual can help himself to more healthful living.

Dr. Cooper's research will continue; and it will help to unravel the mysteries of exercise physiology and to delineate the role of exercise in the achievement and maintenance of good physical condition. I am confident he is on the right track.

1: The Problem

FOLLOWING ONE of my lectures to a group of physicians a few years ago, I was stopped in the corridor by one of them and asked a question I had been asked many times before.

"I tell some of my inactive patients they should get more exercise," he said earnestly, "and usually suggest something mild, like walking, to get them started. But, when they ask me how much or how long, I'm stumped. I don't know how much is enough, do you?"

I didn't, but the problem had bothered me, too. Most of the medical world, notably in the last decade, has come to recognize the value of exercise not only in maintaining a healthy body, but as therapy for unhealthy bodies. Vigorous activity has more and more proved worthwhile both as preventive medicine and as a cure. Little has been done, however, to measure its effects scientifically. Just how much exercise is enough? At what point do the benefits begin? And as the body improves, how do you measure the improvement?

We've had patients who entered, voluntarily, into exercise programs and then came back six months or a year later to report how much better they felt. Six months! One year! Exactly when did they start feeling better? Or, to be more scientific, at what point did they actually become better? The results could be measured, but not the progress. What's more important, it was not possible to give anyone a graded program of exercise based on actually measured data.

We've had other patients who needed such a program.

They'd begin, then quit within a few weeks. I believe now, as I believed then, that they gave up mentally before they gave up physically. They had no standards to aim at, and progress is hard to measure in such a void. They asked the same question my physician friend asked, "How much is enough?" Getting no anwer, they became discouraged.

Well, this problem plagued me, and the more I thought about it, the more I felt that what was needed in the field of exercise was a *pharmacopeia*, a catalog of all the popular forms of activity reduced to measurable amounts, so that anyone could pick and choose among them and know how much exercise would be necessary to produce a beneficial effect.

The more I pondered the question, the more I felt I was in a unique position to do something about it.

Having come from a family of active people who went into medicine, I grew up in an atmosphere in which the importance of regular exercise was emphasized. After medical school, I did graduate work in the field of exercise physiology. However, what brought it all into focus was the opportunity afforded me by the United States Air Force. After entering the service, my assignment, among other duties, was to determine the effects of exercise on the human body, especially as it affected pilots and astronauts. The Air Force's mission has always revolved around its flying personnel and, with its Manned Orbital Laboratory (MOL) program, it is now getting into the space age. However, as any employer in a large organization knows, the entire work force is important. It takes time and money to train a man, whether it's to fly a jet or to repair an engine or to work at a desk, and if you lose him to illness it takes more time and money to train another man to replace him.

I have been able to use the most modern and sophisticated testing equipment in the field of exercise physiology, including some developed by space-age technology. I have also had available an almost unlimited supply of the most priceless research commodity of all—the human body, in the form of the Air Force population.

At this writing, we have evaluated, in one form or another, more than 5000 subjects. These include officers and airmen, pilots and astronauts, athletes and nonathletes, the active and the inactive, the healthy and the unhealthy, and men and women—both in the field and in the laboratory. The discoveries and breakthroughs made in these tests, and the refinements in existing data, have given us enormous amounts of data on how exercise, or the lack of it, affects the body.

As word of our formal evaluation programs spread, informal inquiries and volunteers came flocking in. I'd always known there was a groundswell of interest in the subject, if someone could give it direction, but it came sooner and was stronger than I expected. What started out as a research project, gradually grew into an operational program.

The initial inquiry came from Colonel John Buckner, the dynamic commandant of the Squadron Officers' School (SOS) at Maxwell Air Force Base, Alabama. He first asked me to evaluate the school's physical fitness program, then lecture on my theories of exercise to the students—mostly men in their late 20s taking special training to assume executive positions at the squadron level. This sort of inquiry spread to other groups and age levels, including the Air Command and Staff College (ACSC) at Maxwell, the basic-training recruits at Lackland Air Force Base, Texas, and the MOL astronauts at the Space Systems Division in Los Angeles, California. Several Air National Guard groups began programs, and a few former colleagues, who left the service to specialize in preventive medicine, stopped by to pick up complete details.

We received statistical data from all these organizations, which was what we were interested in primarily, but what delights the heart of any researcher is to see the results take shape before his eyes. It happened to me. After we got started, my office became the haven for all types of personnel, men drawn there on their own or men referred to me by their physicians.

"I heard you had an exercise program going on down here," was a typical opener.

Most, of course, were just inactive types with guilty consciences who needed the impetus of a formal program to jar them into action.

Others were "healthy eaters" whose only exercise was moving from the table to the television set and back again.

A lot were the two-packs-a-day smokers.

And some few were drinkers.

And then there were the nervous types, the insomniacs, whose jobs were chewing holes in them.

One recruit summed up his condition colorfully. "Man, I am just an overweight, over-anxious, chain-smoking slob."

He fit the pattern, too much food, too much stress, too much nicotine and too little activity.

Results?

With the inevitable exceptions, the men who had weight to lose, lost it, or changed fat to muscle and took inches off their waistlines.

The smokers quit or cut down. "Don't need it as much any more."

The drinkers found that exercise relieves tensions as much as a Manhattan.

And, in chorus, they exclaimed they felt better, were more relaxed and were eating less but enjoying it more. The most typical comment was, "I can do more work now with less fatigue, and I sleep like a rock."

Beyond any of this, however, was the hard evidence, as recorded on our testing equipment, that most of them catapulted from the lower 30 percent of the population, in terms of fitness, to the upper 20 percent. There are a few of them I'd match against athletes of comparable age anywhere in the country—and all this from "overweight, over-anxious, chain-smoking slobs."

In fact, we had so many running around our shop in gym clothes that they became known locally as "Cooper's Poopers' Club," and we gave out "roadrunner" decals and tie pins as awards. And some of the prize members of our club were men who had crossed the borderline between the healthy and the unhealthy before joining.

These were the sad cases, especially the pilots. It's bad enough for any man in any job to find he has some disabling ailment, but you have to be around flyers for a while to understand what it means to a man to be grounded because of the development of some medical problem. It can really shake him up.

So it was not at all unusual to come to work some mornings and see one of these grounded pilots sitting on the bench outside my door, a forlorn look on his face. Before he even asked, "Are you Dr. Cooper?" I could tell what he wanted. Others would come during the day, gym shoes under their arm and, with some hesitancy, tell me, "Dr. Smith sent me over. Said you might be able to help."

Among those we helped were:

Some with diabetes.

Some with ulcers.

Some with lung ailments.

Some with arthritis.

Many with cardiovascular conditions, ranging from rheumatic fever, high blood pressure, congenital heart disease and rhythm irregularities, to outright coronaries. Needless to say, *all were required to have clearances from their physicians.* In fact, most were sent to us by their physicians.

And we had another type that is hard to define, but the symptoms were clear: The depressed.

I'll give you medical detail on most of these later, but it's safe to say here that, almost without exception, they showed remarkable improvement after they entered the program. Some were outstanding cases. A few set medical precedents.

In general, most of the diabetics were able to reduce or eliminate medication. The stomach ulcers became less symptomatic. The lung ailments improved. In at least one case, the symptoms of arthritis disappeared, and nearly all of the cardiovascular cases consistently showed improvement.

The physical rehabilitation, however, was secondary to the personality rehabilitation. This change in their personalities was manifested by the loss of anxiety and the acquisition of the ability to relax. They had a better self-image and more confidence in themselves. Introverts became extroverts. In fact, one of my biggest problems after I got them into shape was how to get rid of them. All they wanted to do was talk about exercise! But they're a tremendous group and the time was certainly well spent.

Among the failures, and we had some, the only common denominator I could find was lack of motivation. As the boys down on the flight line would say, "They just couldn't hack it."

All of which brings us down to you.

If you can "hack it," if you've got the proper motivation, if you're truly concerned about getting your body into condition and keeping it there, I can give you a program of exercise that will match whatever motivation you bring to it.

This program has been tested to exhaustion, by the most modern means available, both in the field and in the laboratory. And it has been proved several thousand times over in the only place it really counts—in the human body.

There's only one problem remaining. I can give you the

program, but I can't do it for you. You have to do the rest. It isn't easy, but it works. Keep this in mind whenever you think about quitting: it's medically sound and it works.

Briefly, the program goes something like this.

All popular exercises have been scientifically measured for the amount of energy it costs the body to perform them. These amounts have been translated into points—the more energy it costs, the more points, less energy, less points—and the number of points necessary to produce an optimum level of fitness has been firmly established by our evaluations. Earn that basic minimum every week, by whatever combination of exercise you choose, and you will be answering the basic question, "How much?"

To begin, I will give you a simple field test to perform that will establish your present physical condition. The test, a direct translation of those we perform in our laboratory, is important because it's dangerous to start into an exercise program too fast. The test will place you in one of several basic categories of fitness, each with its own graduated rate of progress.

Next, after you have established your category, you can begin one of the conditioning programs to work your way gradually back into top shape. If you have no serious ailments, you should begin getting solid results within eight weeks and you should be in good condition within 16 weeks at the most. If you have a clinical condition, requiring doctor's care, progress will—and should—be much slower.

Finally, after you have completed one of the conditioning programs, and have worked your body back into condition, you can then go to the point chart, the *pharmacopeia*, and choose whatever assortment of exercises that will earn you enough points weekly to keep you in condition, from now until your dotage.

Simple enough?

The beauty of the system is that it allows you to choose your own form of exercise, secure in the knowledge that if you do enough exercise—earn enough points—there is a scientific basis for measuring the medical benefits.

As one of Cooper's Poopers put it, "I used to exercise and stop whenever I felt like it. Now I've got something worthwhile to aim at."

Now you've got something to aim at.

Good Luck!

2: The Key

I PROMISED some explanations.

The first is the basis of the point system, and the best way to explain it is to tell you of an incident that happened to me not long ago. I was visiting a colleague who was testing volunteers for a special project that would require men in the best possible condition. I passed three of the volunteers in the hall. Two had normal builds, but the third was definitely muscular.

"Which of the three do you think will get our recommendation?" my friend asked, tossing their medical records across the desk. I skimmed over the physiological data until I came to the slot where it asked, "Regular exercise?"

One wrote, candidly, "None."

The second, "Nothing regular. Just ride my bike to the base and back every day. About three miles one way."

The third, "Isometrics and weight lifting, one hour a day, five days a week." The muscular one!

I glanced back over each of the records. All pilots, all in their early 30s, none with any history of illness.

"Well?" asked my friend.

"I'd bet on the cyclist."

"Not the weight lifter?"

"Not if that's all he does."

My friend smiled. "I think you're right."

Next day he proved it. The three came back for their treadmill tests and the nonexerciser and the weight lifter were completely fatigued within the first five minutes. The cyclist was still going strong 10 minutes later, running uphill at a 6½ mph clip. He was recommended for the project. The other two weren't.

This story, when I use it in my lectures, always surprises people. The nonexerciser they can believe. The cyclist, maybe. But the weight lifter, or anyone who does strictly isometrics or calisthenics, they all *look* in such good condition!

In my business, looks are deceitful. Some exceptionally physically fit men tested in our laboratory were middle-aged types with slight builds, including an occasional one with a paunch. Some of the most unfit we've ever seen were husky young men with cardiac conditions.

If this shatters any illusions about slim waistlines and large biceps being the key to good health, I'm sorry. They're not a deterrent, but they're no guarantee either. They're mostly a byproduct. The real key is elsewhere.

Take those three volunteers. By ordinary standards, all three should have been accepted. None of them had any physical defects, or ever had any. Why the discrimination?

For special projects, the military services can afford to be discriminate. They can afford to classify the physically fit into their three classic categories and choose only the most fit.

The nonexerciser represents passive fitness. There's nothing wrong with him—not yet anyway—but there's nothing really right with him either. If he's lucky, he can coast like that for years. But, without any activity, his body is essentially deteriorating.

The weight lifter, or those who emphasize isometrics or calisthenics, represent muscular fitness. These types, who have the right motives but the wrong approach, are stuck with the myth that muscular strength or agility means physical fitness. This is one of the great misconceptions in the field of exercise. The muscles that show—the skeletal muscles—are just one system in the body, and by no means the most important. If your exercise program is directed only at the skeletal muscles, you'll never achieve real physical fitness.

The cyclist, whether he knew it or not, had found one of the most basic means to overall fitness. According to my point chart, by riding three miles to work, six miles round trip, he was earning more than enough points to answer the question, "How much exercise?" And he proved it on the treadmill.

The cyclist represents the third, and best, kind of fitness, overall fitness. We call it endurance fitness, or working capacity, the ability to do prolonged work without undue fatigue. It assumes the absence of any ailment, and it has little to do with pure muscular strength or agility. It has very much to do with the body's *overall* health, the health of the heart, the lungs, the entire cardiovascular system and the other organs, *as well as* the muscles.

And the key to the whole thing is oxygen.

Let me explain.

In its simplest terms, any activity requires energy. The body produces energy by burning foodstuffs. The burning agent is oxygen. Even down at Cape Kennedy, the rocket boosters carry fuel and an oxidizer to burn it for energy. Once they leave the atmosphere they run out of natural oxygen so they have to carry it with them. Aircraft, which stay within the atmosphere, use the oxygen in the air to burn their fuel. In the body, the fuel is food and the flame is oxygen.

Now comes the problem. The body can store food, *but it can't store oxygen.* Eating three times a day is more than enough for most of us; the body uses what it wants and saves some of the rest for later. Not so with oxygen. It needs to replenish its supply constantly, so we breathe in and out every moment of our lives to keep the supply coming in. If the supply were suddenly cut off, the oxygen stored in the body wouldn't last more than a few minutes. The brain, the heart, everything would cease functioning.

But since we live within the atmosphere, the supply of oxygen is unlimited. If we need more, we just breathe more. So what's the problem?

The problem is to get enough oxygen to all the areas—all the small, hidden, infinite areas in this wonderful mechanism we call the human body—where the food is stored, so that the two can combine to produce enough energy.

This is what separates the men from the boys, the fit from the unfit. *Because, in some bodies, the means for delivering the oxygen is weak and limited in its resources, so the energy demands surpass the body's capacity to produce it.*

Most of us can produce enough energy to perform ordinary daily activities. However, as the activities become more vigorous, some of us can't keep up.

This spread, this difference between our *minimum requirements* and our *maximum capacity,* is the measure of our fitness. The most physically fit have the greatest spread; the least fit, the lowest spread. In some, the minimum and maximum are almost identical.

Take yourself. What are you doing right now? Sitting down? All right, let's start there. You're relatively inactive now so no energy is required. Right? Wrong!

Sitting, or even sleeping, the body is burning foodstuffs for energy, and bringing in oxygen to do the burning. Otherwise, we could stop breathing temporarily. Even sleeping, energy is required for the heart to beat, for the digestive system to function, for body temperature to be maintained, and even for the lungs to bring in the oxygen! So the body is constantly in need of energy. It becomes a question of how much energy is required and how much oxygen you can bring in and deliver to produce it.

Let's get back to the sitting position, and consider you along with those three Air Force volunteers, the nonexerciser, the weight lifter and the cyclist. If the cyclist is in better condition, he should require more energy right now. Right? Wrong!

For any given activity, the energy requirements are comparable for everyone, with some variation for body size and physical condition. This is the basis of our point system. We measure the activity and the energy required, average the results, then translate it into points that are applicable for all, fit or unfit. As the four of you sit there, you each require about the same amount of energy and consume the same amount of oxygen.

But let's go on. Get up from your chair. That mild exertion cost a little more energy and a little more oxygen. Now start walking. Still more energy and still more oxygen. Now all four of you go outdoors and start running. You'll stay together for a while, using equal amounts of energy and equal amounts of oxygen, but you can begin to see what's going to happen. One by one you'll start dropping back, as each of your bodies reaches the point where it can't supply all the oxygen for the energy demanded. In short, each of you, sooner or later, reaches the point of exhaustion. For those with small reserves, with a small spread between their minimum daily energy requirements and their maximum capacity, the point of exhaustion comes much sooner. For those with large reserves, with a large spread between their minimum requirements and maximum capacity, it comes much later.

You know where you'd start dropping back, or quitting altogether. But look at what your body is doing in its noble effort to keep you going. Your chest is heaving as the lungs try to bring in more oxygen. Your heart is pounding as it tries to pump more blood (which carries the oxygen) around the body. And the blood is racing through the blood vessels to every extremity as it tries to deliver more oxygen.

It's the condition of these systems and others which determines your endurance fitness, and it's the improvement of these systems toward which all exercise should be directed.

Now for everybody's favorite argument:

"Doc, I don't need much endurance. I work at a desk all day, and I watch television at night. I don't exert myself any more than I have to, and I have no requirements for exerting myself. Who needs large reserves? Who needs endurance?"

You do. Everyone does.

Surely you know the usual symptoms caused by inactivity as well as I do. Yawning at your desk, that drowsy feeling all day, falling asleep after a heavy meal, fatigue from even mild exertions like climbing stairs, running for a bus, mowing the lawn or shoveling the snow. You can become a social cripple, "too tired" to play with the kids, "too tired" to go out to dinner with your wife, "too tired" to do anything except sit at your desk or watch television, and maybe you're even getting tired doing that. And the final clincher, "I guess I'm getting old."

You're getting old all right, and a lot sooner than you should.

Most of the medical symptoms caused by inactivity are well known and they are alarming. A body that isn't used deteriorates. The lungs become inefficient, the heart grows weaker, the blood vessels less pliable, the muscles lose tone and the body generally weakens throughout, leaving it vulnerable for a whole catalog of illness and disease. Your whole system for delivering oxygen almost literally shrivels up.

And, if you compound the felony of inactivity by smoking two packs of cigarettes a day, by eating anything in sight, and by worrying about everything else—including your health—then the only advice I can give you is to keep up the payments on your insurance, if you can get any.

Endurance, however, is the best kind of insurance.

If you'd like to develop some, if you'd like to start back down that road toward physical fitness, then get active with the kind of exercises that will demand oxygen and force your body to process and deliver it. Even if you've crossed the borderline between the well and the unwell, *and have your own doctor's permission and encouragement*, I can recommend no greater therapy. And, if you follow the point system and get enough of the right kind of exercise, it will produce many wonderful changes in your body that are cumulatively known as the "training effect."

This is a phrase I will use repeatedly throughout this book, so it is important to understand it now. The training effect is the whole goal of endurance exercise. The point system is a means for measuring the training to assure that you get enough.

I will go into more complete detail later, but these are some of the highlights:

• The training effect increases the efficiency of the lungs, conditioning them to process more air with less effort. During exhausting work, a conditioned man may process nearly twice as much air per minute as a deconditioned man, providing his body with more oxygen for the energy-producing process.

• The training effect increases the efficiency of the heart in several ways. It grows stronger and pumps more blood with each stroke, reducing the number of strokes necessary. A conditioned man may have a resting heart rate 20 beats per minute slower than a deconditioned man, saving as many as 10,000 beats in one night's sleep. Even during maximum exertion, a conditioned heart can pump all the blood (and oxygen) the body needs at much lower rates than a deconditioned heart. In contrast, a deconditioned heart may pump dangerously fast during maximum exertion in its attempt to deliver enough oxygen.

• The training effect increases the number and size of the blood vessels that carry the blood to the body tissue, saturating the tissue throughout the body with energy-producing oxygen.

• The training effect increases the total blood volume, again providing more means for delivering more oxygen to the body tissue.

• The training effect improves the tone of the muscles and blood vessels, changing them from weak and flabby tissue to strong and firm tissue, often reducing blood pressure in the process.

• The training effect changes fat weight to lean weight, often toughening up the body without actual weight loss.

• The training effect increases maximal oxygen consumption by increasing the efficiency of the means of supply and delivery. In the very act of doing so, it is improving the overall condition of the body, especially its most important parts, the lungs, the heart, the blood vessels and the body tissue, building a bulwark against many forms of illness and disease.

None of this is idle speculation. All of it is evidence gathered in laboratories under scientific conditions as effects of endurance training.

There are other benefits to the training effect that are harder to document because they are all subjective. But, if Cooper's Poopers' and a few thousand other opinions are worth anything, here are some of them.

• The training effect may change your whole outlook on life. You'll learn to relax, develop a better self-image, be able to tolerate the stress of daily living better. And, what is very important, you'll sleep better and get more work done with less fatigue, including desk work.

To summarize what I've been saying:

Passive fitness, the mere absence of any illness, is a losing battle. Without activity, the body begins to deteriorate and appears to become more vulnerable to certain chronic illnesses and diseases.

Muscular fitness is of some value, but it is too limited. It concentrates on only one system in the body, one of the least important ones, and has limited beneficial effect on the essential organs or overall health. It's like putting a lovely new coat of paint on an automobile that really needs an engine overhaul.

Endurance fitness should be your goal. It will assure all the benefits of the training effect, improving not just your muscles, but your lungs, your heart, and your blood vessels. It is the foundation on which all forms of fitness should be built.

The key to endurance training is oxygen consumption. The body needs it to produce energy. It can't store it, so it must bring it in constantly and deliver it to the organ or tissue where the energy is needed. The amount that the body can bring in and deliver—your maximum oxygen consumption —is the best measure of your fitness.

Each exercise requires a certain amount of energy, consequently a certain amount of oxygen. This oxygen requirement can be measured, and this is the basis of the point system. Each exercise is assigned a certain number of points, based on the amount of oxygen required to perform it.

If you earn enough points you will begin reaping the benefits of the training effect and raising the level of your fitness, raising your maximum oxygen consumption, and spreading the gap between your minimum requirements and what you can deliver in emergencies.

All set?

Then let's get to the exercises.

3: The Exercises

IT MAY surprise you to learn that there is nothing exotic about any of the exercises used in this program. I didn't create any new ones—just measured the old ones.

It may disappoint you to learn that some of your favorites didn't do so well.

It may shock you to learn that some exercises don't make the list at all.

Most of the old standbys are here, however, the pure exercises done just for the sake of exercise, and the participant sports done for the sake of enjoyment, with exercise a beneficial byproduct. What happened to the others is that some of them had such a low oxygen requirement that in order to reap a beneficial training effect, you'd have to spend hours doing them. The remainder of the exercises built up an "oxygen debt" so rapidly that they were almost worthless.

I'll state my position early. The best exercises are running, swimming, cycling, walking, stationary running, handball, basketball and squash, and in just about that order.

Isometrics, weight lifting and calisthenics, though good as far as they go, don't even make the list, despite the fact that most exercise books are *based* on one of these three, especially calisthenics.

Participant sports, like golf, tennis, volleyball and others, fall somewhere in between, not as good as the first group, but definitely better than the second.

Those exercises which didn't make the list at all were excluded because we were unable to show any appreciable training effect from their use.

There are two basic reasons for this. Either the exercise is aimed solely at the skeletal muscles, and consequently makes little or no demands on the lungs, heart and blood system, or the exercise is done for such a short time that these organs never reach a "steady state" of exertion where the training-effect benefits begin.

There is no way I know of to lift a strict muscle-producing exercise into an oxygen-demanding activity so that it can produce a training effect and earn points, but there is a secret to changing those short, stop-and-go exercises into more worthwhile point-earning activities. I'll explain how further on.

For the moment, I just want to impress upon you, backed by all the data collected, that when I tell you this particular exercise is a good one and that particular exercise is not nearly as good for building true fitness, I really have no choice. The evidence is before me.

I'd now like to explain some of that evidence.

I'll begin by breaking down exercise into its four basic categories:

Those that tense muscles without producing movement, while demanding little or no oxygen;

Those that tense muscles to produce movement without demanding much oxygen;

Those that demand a lot of oxygen but are over too quickly to produce a definite training effect; and

Those that demand sufficient oxygen and last long enough to produce a definite training effect.

ISOMETRICS

(Literally, "equal measure.") Isometric exercises contract muscles without producing movement or demanding appreciable amounts of oxygen. Generally, they tense one set of muscles against another or against an immovable object. Examples are pushing against opposite sides of a doorjamb, or pulling up on the chair you're sitting on.

Isometrics have received a lot of publicity in recent years, but actually, they're not new. Serious medical experiments go back at least to the 1920s when therapists used them to maintain strength in patients whose limbs were enclosed in casts. The recent rash of isometric fervor, however, probably grew from an English translation of some German experiments, published in 1952, which concluded that isometric contractions could increase the size and strength of the muscles by as much as five percent a week. While both the experiments and the translation were done in good faith by respected men of medicine, the conclusions reached were later modified or disproved.

Serious researchers and therapists continued to study isometrics and define their limits, but no one paid much attention to them. Momentum increased and the interest in "instant exercise" reached a high level. People were anxious to hear about a guaranteed shortcut to fitness consisting of "sixty seconds of exercise a day that wouldn't produce sweat." Isometrics thus became the most abused, and least understood, of all exercises.

I'd like to settle this once and for all. No one has ever been able to show a measurable training effect from exercising just 60 seconds a day, regardless of the type.

Needless to say, the medical world, in particular the men who may have been indirectly responsible for the isometric fad, were, and are, a little dismayed at this perversion of an otherwise useful tool!

Let me elaborate a little more. Isometric exercises are capable of increasing the size and strength of individual skeletal muscles, but they have no significant effect on overall health, especially on the pulmonary and cardiovascular systems. There is no increase in oxygen consumption and, consequently, minimal if any training effect.

At best, isometrics have some effect on body building, chiefly the limbs, if that is your goal. They are more valuable, however, in therapeutics. Bedridden patients can use them to prevent atrophy (wasting away) in unused muscles, and even the astronauts, believe it or not, can maintain strength in some muscles on long space voyages when other forms of exercise are too awkward or impossible in a weightless state.

But since isometrics affect only the skeletal muscles, they do not strengthen the heart, the lungs or the blood system ... And any claims that they can keep you fit in "sixty seconds a day" are not scientifically sound.

Try it. Go over to a doorjamb and push as hard as you can for a few seconds. Now, is your chest heaving, is your heart pounding, is the blood racing around your system trying to deliver more and more oxygen?

Nonsense, none of these beneficial things is going on, nothing that anyone can measure, anyway. We tried it and failed.

Furthermore, since isometrics work on only one muscle group at a time, even if larger muscles were your goal you would spend considerably more than 60 seconds a day before you got around to all of them. Some researchers claim if you did get around to all of them your tongue would be hanging out further than if you had devoted the same time to other, more worthwhile exercises. You would have reached exhaustion without the reciprocal benefits of exhaustion.

Then there is the problem of motivation. Just how tense is tense? It varies with individuals, the more conscientious putting more effort into it, the less conscientious, less. The researchers claim you must put more than two-thirds of your maximum strength into each exercise and hold it at least six seconds; and there is no way for the average man to measure "two-thirds" of his strength or to measure the results. Runners run faster or farther and weight lifters add more weight as they improve; but how do you measure improvement in isometrics without special equipment?

Perhaps the worst fault of isometrics, however, is that they do not demand enough oxygen to produce a significant training effect. They build bigger muscles, but there is no evidence to indicate that the blood supply to them improves. Therefore, during sustained effort these muscles are easily fatigued. There is such a thing as being overmuscled as well as overfat. In either case, extra weight is being imposed on a cardiovascular system that has not been trained to support it.

Also, isometric exercises may make a joint more vulnerable to injury. At least one college football team, the Arkansas Razorbacks, and one professional team, the New York Giants, tried and then discarded isometric exercises when a rash of knee injuries, many requiring surgery, sidelined some of their players.

Finally, I personally question whether the increase in strength claimed for isometrics, which seems to be their only virtue, is actually useful strength. Static contraction of a muscle in only one direction produces only one-dimensional strength, strength that would be useless for work in other dimensions. If isometrics could increase strength simply by static contraction, this same strength could be produced by using electrical stimulation to contract the muscles. It has been tried in laboratories and it hasn't worked.

As you've probably gathered by now, I don't have much respect for isometrics, or any short-cut program, as a means to overall fitness. Besides doing little that's worthwhile for the body, they delude you into thinking you're fitter than you are. Except for their therapeutic value in specialized cases, isometrics seem to have little benefit for the average person.

In summary, I would define isometrics as great exercises for developing muscles to do isometrics—and little else.

ISOTONICS

(Literally, "equal tension.") Isotonic exercises contract muscles and produce movement. Popular examples are calisthenics and weight lifting, and some of the mild participant sports like shuffleboard, archery and horseshoes.

None of these makes very much demand on the oxygen-consumption process, so none of them scores points. They are aimed almost entirely at the skeletal muscles.

If nothing else, however, isotonics are preferable to isometrics because they exercise muscles over a range of motion. They are dynamic or three-dimensional exercises, as opposed to static, one-dimensional exercises.

I will probably get some very large arguments about calisthenics. In fact, I already have.

"Doc, I can remember when I was doing calisthenics regularly, and I can remember huffing and puffing like a steam engine after some of them."

Some of them? And how long?

See, we're back to the two basic drawbacks, some of them are all-muscle exercises, and *don't* make you huff and puff, and others are too-short exercises and never get to the point where the huffing and puffing can do you some good.

I do calisthenics myself, but I earn my points elsewhere. I can't justify taking points for something I know is producing little or no training effect. The evidence is with me.

Try some.

Try touching your toes 25 or 30 times. (Why 25 or 30? I haven't the slightest idea, but those are the figures most of the exercise books use.) Are you breathing hard? I doubt it.

Try 25 or 30 situps, bringing your knees up to your chest each time. Breathing harder? Perhaps.

Now 25 or 30 pushups. Most people can't make that many, but even when their strength gives out—their *muscular* strength—they still aren't breathing appreciably harder than when at rest.

Are you? Even if you are, there's the second factor.

Twenty-five or 30 pushups don't last long enough to enable your body to reach that "steady state" required to produce a training effect. If it were possible to achieve a training effect exercising exclusively with calisthenics, it would probably be necessary to continuously perform calisthenics at a very rapid rate for a minimum of a half hour every day.

Those are the three calisthenics I recommend most often, not for points, but just to keep a few muscle groups loosened up and to maintain their strength and tone. The principal ones are the back muscles (very important, especially as you grow older!), the abdominal muscles and the arms and shoulders. There are other calisthenics, some a little more vigorous, some a little less. The ones I find hard to recommend, especially for older people, are those that require agility. You can strain muscles, principally around joints, and for no useful purpose.

Calisthenics, then, should not be considered the foundation of any exercise program. They're just the bricks that go on top.

Weight lifters also give me a hard time; but their arguments are even less valid than those who defend calisthenics. While calisthenics can develop your muscles along the natural lines of the body you were born with—slimming you down where you should be slim and building you up where you should be built—weight lifting goes beyond this, building you up to an unnatural degree. It's definitely aimed at the muscles, and it has but little training effect on the heart and lungs. How much better to devote some of that time and effort to building true fitness in the heart and lungs!

If you lay these on top of the endurance-producing exercises, you'll be on reasonably safe ground. You'll be building up your essential systems that will have to support your new muscles.

Then there are the bowlers. I'd have to be a pretty brave man to knock an activity that is one of the most popular competitive sports in the country. I'm reasonably brave, but I'm not knocking it. Any activity that gives you some pleasure is worthwhile. Just don't think of it as a basic exercise. It isn't.

Let me illustrate what I mean. If you get up from your seat, walk over to the rack and pick up a 16-pound ball, take a few short steps and roll the ball down the alley, does this make your chest heave, your heart pound and your blood race around your system? The answer is certainly no! It's all over too fast. Three hours of this may give you some physical benefit, and score you a minimum number of points, but it's by no means a basic conditioner.

Isotonics, then, are basically muscle exercises, some of them worth more than others, but none of them qualifies as a primary conditioner.

ANAEROBICS

(Literally, "without oxygen.") Anaerobics fall into two classes, those that demand reasonable amounts of oxygen but are cut short voluntarily, and those that demand exorbitant amounts of oxygen and are cut short involuntarily. The body just can't take it.

An example of the first is any exercise that can make you "huff and puff," but is usually over too quickly for the "steady state" to be established, like running for a short distance, cycling a few blocks, swimming a few laps, or walking to the corner drugstore.

An example of the second is any exercise that demands so much oxygen in so short a time that the heart and lungs can't possibly supply it, thus creating an "oxygen debt" that must be paid quickly. And the only way to pay it is to stop and recover. Wind sprints, interval training, the 100-yard dash, swimming and bicycle sprints all qualify.

Exercises like these that rapidly create large oxygen debts are used during practice by competitive athletes to build up speed. They have no place in an ordinary physical-fitness program.

Exercises that demand oxygen, without creating a large oxygen debt, are the kind on which you should concentrate;

but they must be kept up long enough to do you some good. Those few steps you take running for a bus won't do it, neither will most of the calisthenics. They end too soon. A notable exception is running-in-place, which can be kept up nonstop for a considerable length of time, demanding oxygen all the while.

So, in general, anaerobics are not for you. The least vigorous ones, like that short walk to the corner drugstore, won't produce a training effect, and the most vigorous ones, like wind sprints, could kill you. Even if they didn't, they would be over too quickly to benefit your body.

There are other exercises, however, like running in place, that lift themselves out of the isotonic and anaerobic categories and definitely produce a training effect.

Let's meet them.

AEROBICS

(Literally, "with oxygen.") These are the foundation exercises on which any exercise program should be built. These exercises demand oxygen without producing an intolerable oxygen debt, so that they can be continued for long periods. They activate the training effect and start producing all those wonderful changes in your body.

Your lungs begin processing more air and with less effort, your heart grows stronger, pumping more blood with fewer strokes, the blood supply to your muscles improves, and your total blood volume increases.

In short, you are improving your body's capacity to bring in oxygen and deliver it to the tissue cells where it is combined with foodstuffs to produce energy.

You are increasing your oxygen consumption and, consequently, your endurance capacity.

If the word endurance still scares you, it shouldn't. You don't have to enter the Boston Marathon, or swim the English Channel or compete in a six-day bicycle race to develop endurance. In fact, you don't have to run, swim or ride a bike at all. There are many popular sports and exercises, better than bowling and calisthenics, and almost as good as running, swimming and cycling, that can produce training effects.

Some of them, you may have noticed, overlap several exercise categories. Golf is a good example.

You take your stance, line up the shot, then, just before swinging, grip the club tightly and tense your arms. (Isometrics.)

Next, you swing, moving your arms, shoulders and hips. (Isotonics.)

Then you start walking after the ball. (Anaerobics.)

After five hours of that you've walked well past the point where anaerobics leave off and aerobics begin.

However please note where the aerobic effect began. Not in tensing your muscles or in moving them (both trivial), not in walking short distances, but in walking probably more than 6000 yards, about 3½ miles, up and down hills.

Where, then, does endurance start? Where do the training-effect benefits actually begin?

After four years of searching for it, I can lay down two basic principles. If your program is limited to 12-20 minutes a day of activity, the exercise must be vigorous enough to produce a sustained heart rate of 150 beats per minute or more. If the exercise is not vigorous enough to produce a sustained heart rate of 150 beats per minute, but is still demanding oxygen, the exercise must be continued longer than 20 minutes, the total period of time depending on the oxygen consumed.

I can see I've furrowed your brow. How in the world can any man figure out his heart rate while he's in the act of exercising?

That is the beauty of the point system. All the figuring has been done for you.

I took most of the exercises that we know demand oxygen —aerobically, not anaerobically—and we measured them for the amount of oxygen they require. We translated this amount into points.

Some, obviously, are more vigorous and require more oxygen to produce the needed energy and so were awarded more points.

Running is the best example.

Some are less vigorous and require less oxygen to produce the needed energy and so were awarded fewer points.

Some are vigorous but too intermittent to rate the same number of points as a nonstop exercise like running. Tennis and handball, for instance. You dash about the court chasing the ball, and the heart rate goes up to 150 or more. A point is scored and the action stops. The heart rate comes down to 120 or less. After a few games like this, the *average* heart rate is less than the 150 produced by nonstop aerobics. There is a definite aerobic benefit, but the point value levels out somewhere between running and walking.

The complete point chart, with all the exercises, is on page 20 of the center section, but I'd like to give you some comparative examples here. Each of these exercises is comparable in its aerobic training effect.

> Running 1 mile in less than 8 minutes
> Swimming 24 laps (600 yards) in less than 15 minutes
> Cycling 5 miles in less than 20 minutes
> Stationary running for a total of 12½ minutes
> Handball played for a total of 35 minutes

All are worth five points. Any of them done daily, six times a week, would give you all the exercise you need (30 points) to produce and maintain a beautiful training effect in your body. In fact, I even like the mixture. There's a lot to be said for variety, for choosing different exercises to earn the same number of points. A week of running, swimming, cycling, handball and walking could hardly become monotonous.

However, there's nothing mandatory about these or any other set of exercises, nor about exercising six days a week. The only other principle we've laid down, based on our findings, is that you must maintain a minimum of 30 points a week and exercise at least four times a week, or every other day. The training-effect benefits start dropping off if you fall below either minimum. Don't, for instance, try to earn 30 points in one day, then skip exercising for the next six. Something trivial done every day is just as useless. You've got to earn 30 points, spread over at least four days.

But the choice of how you earn them is yours. That, again, is the unique aspect of the point system. Find the point value of each exercise you plan to use and exercise enough to earn 30 points. Five points one day, one point the next, nine the next, and so on, as long as they all add up to 30. In between days of formal exercise, you can pick up points just walking.

You'll note when you study the point chart that different lengths of time for the same exercise score different points.

Swimming 24 laps in less than 15 minutes scores five points. If it takes 21 minutes, you earn only 1½ points. Why?

The times, distances and energy required are all figured into the number of points awarded for each exercise. If you are doing 24 laps in 21 minutes, speed it up and try to do them in 15 minutes. You'll find out in a hurry how much extra energy it takes to cut the time down, and you probably won't be able to do it the first few times.

Once you make it, however, you will definitely be earning those five points. Your body will have made the necessary adjustments (the training effect!) to move that oxygen rapidly to the place where it's needed, so the energy required for that extra effort can be provided.

So we always come back to the same thing. The effect you get from the exercise you select depends upon the type, the duration, and the effort you put into it.

If you were to ask me, finally, what exercise can be used most effectively, I'd have no hesitancy about recommending running. Cooper's Poopers' Club uses it exclusively. So do I.

As one of the Poopers put it, "It's like a dry martini. You get more for your money—and quicker!"

I'd have chosen a different analogy, but his point is valid. You definitely do get more benefit—and quicker—from running than from any other form of exercise. Look at the examples—five points in eight minutes! You get more benefit from this than you do from seven hours of golf!

Your argument, of course, might be that you enjoy golf.

Fine. Enjoy your golf, and pick up a few points. Pick them up any way that suits you best.

Exercise can be used in many ways and you have to decide what you want it to do for you.

If it's muscles or a body beautiful, you'll get it from weight lifting or calisthenics, but not much more.

If it's recreation and leisure-time pleasure, you'll get it—and some physical benefit—from golf and tennis, but you'll get more essential benefit from something more vigorous like handball and squash.

If it's the health of your body, you'll get it more quickly from one of the basic aerobic conditioners and more slowly from leisure-time sports.

Once you've made your decision, the course of action is up to you. If it's the overall health of your body you're interested in, isometrics won't do it for you, neither will isotonics, or anaerobics. Aerobic exercises are the only ones that will.

Before you start on them, however, you'd better find out what kind of shape you're in so you won't start too fast.

4: The Test

I DO some wishful thinking from time to time.

One of my most ardent wishes is that, some day, a man can walk in off the street, into a drugstore or a supermarket or some public place, and stick a coin in a machine such as a treadmill or a bicycle ergometer, work out for a few minutes, then get the results of his workout on the spot. A card or a gauge would tell him exactly what kind of physical condition he was in at the moment.

In Europe, they're coming close to that happy state. Europe in general, and the Scandinavian countries in particular, are years ahead of us in the study, promotion and *practice* of exercise as a means toward physical fitness. In Sweden alone, there are more than five hundred bicycle ergometers (stationary bicycles on which the subject pumps against a work load fed into the machine) distributed around the country. And they're not buried in research laboratories, but are available for public use in schools, clinics and factories.

More than 500 of them, in a nation as small as Sweden!

To my knowledge, there isn't one in the United States that the average man could use. The closest public facility we have to a health indicator is the old-fashioned scale.

Weight, while important, is only a superficial indication of the whole health of a man. But how do you find this total picture easily, inexpensively and on the spot? Go to a doctor?

This seems to be the only way, but going to a doctor for

a weekly or monthly checkup is not quite as easy as walking into a drugstore and sticking a coin in a machine. And even doctors will admit that there is no single, *simple* test with which they can consistently and accurately measure the reserve capacity of your heart and lungs.

Several attempts have been devised over the years, and some are still being used; but all fall short of perfection. The "pack test" was developed in the early 1940s for testing military personnel. The soldier was weighed, then given a pack of 40 to 75 pounds, depending on his own weight. With the pack on his back, he was asked to step up and down on a 16-inch stool at the rate of 30 times per minute for five minutes. When he finished, his recovery heart rate was taken during three 30-second intervals. Comparative figures showed which soldiers' hearts recovered more quickly, and basic norms were gradually established.

Similar tests followed. The Harvard step test, which became very popular, used a 20-inch step but eliminated the back pack, exercising the subject longer but less vigorously, again monitoring the recovery heart rate. Masters' two-step test was developed to identify cardiac patients. Other physicians ignored the steps and just had the patient jump up and down or run-in-place to get his heart rate up.

There were other variations on these basic themes, but there were obvious drawbacks to all of them. None was long enough or vigorous enough to really push the subject to a maximum effort, so there were always lingering doubts about what his maximum capacity, or his endurance reserves, really were. A conditioned man and a deconditioned, yet still healthy man might very well produce the same results on short, minimum-effort tests. The heart rate, while essential in any physical examination, is not the best single indicator of overall health. Too many things, especially the emotions, can make test results widely erratic. Tension can make the heart rate accelerate rapidly while the body is at rest, and tension in military physicals is frequently a problem, both to the subject, especially the aircrews, and to the examining flight surgeon. Some physical defects can ground a pilot—and he knows it. So it's always necessary to determine if a rapid heart rate is the result of tension or of some underlying medical problem.

Later, when treadmills and ergometers were introduced,

they eliminated some, but not all of the problems of submaximal efforts. A subject could be pushed to exhaustion on either of them. But even then, the focus of the test was still the heart rate and there was no way to standardize the effect of emotions and other outside influences on the results. One test, called the Physical Working Capacity 150, was developed for use on a bicycle ergometer. No attempt was made to push the subject to exhaustion, but only to determine what work load was necessary to produce a heart rate of 150. On the basis of this performance, estimates of maximal working capacity were then possible from charts. The drawback, again, was that the results varied widely.

It was not until the ergometer and treadmill were combined with oxygen-measuring equipment that these final difficulties were overcome. Tension can make your heart beat faster, but it has practically no effect on oxygen consumption. Either your body can process and consume X-amount of oxygen during maximum effort, or it can't. And that's the most significant fact in the examination.

We have both bicycle ergometers and a treadmill in the laboratory at Wilford Hall Hospital; but we use the treadmill almost exclusively for major evaluations and save the ergometers for special studies. A maximum performance on an ergometer requires unusual leg power that some men, even in the best condition, don't have. And, the ergometer leaves us vulnerable to one particular problem with which I'm sure you're familiar—the malingerer.

If you put a man on a bicycle ergometer, he is furnishing the power to pump against the work load imposed by the machine, either through magnets or springs. Motivation determines whether he pushes himself hard enough to reach a maximum effort.

"Golly, sir, I'm trying the best I can," he cries, with one foot on the floor, one eye on the clock and the other on a nurse who just passed by.

Treadmill testing is less dependent upon motivation. The power is supplied by the machine and the subject is required to keep up with it whether he wants to or not. If he doesn't, he slips off the end and comes to an abrupt, sometimes embarrassing halt.

So treadmill testing is presently the ultimate in measuring total fitness, and it is universally recognized as such by exercise physiologists. Treadmill studies permit an accurate measure of maximal oxygen consumption and a correlation of oxygen consumption with heart rate and blood pressure.

In short, treadmill performance measures maximum endurance capacity—that spread between the energy needs at rest and the total amount of energy the body is able to produce before exhaustion—all of which is an excellent indicator of the overall health of the body, especially of the essential organs, the lungs, the heart and the circulatory system.

I'd like to explain how a treadmill test works. Let's assume you're the subject. Follow along as I describe it.

Preparations would have begun the day before. You would have been asked to get a good night's rest, and to eat lightly and at least three hours prior to the test. This insures that neither fatigue nor the ingestion of too much food would interfere with reaching maximum capacity. Temporary fatigue would make you peak out below maximum.

At the laboratory, you would be asked to put on running clothes and gym shoes. Next you would be weighed; a brief physical examination would be given and a medical history taken. This would include a recent history of your exercise habits so that we could set the treadmill accordingly. A man in good condition can tolerate a higher work load than a man in poor condition. In either case, we have to push him as close to exhaustion as possible and still complete the test.

Assuming you're in good health, we'd start preparing you for the test. First, the electrodes for the electrocardiograph are attached to your chest. This enables us to observe your electrocardiogram (ECG) during the study. If any abnormality develops, the run is stopped immediately.

Next, you are connected to a system enabling us to collect all or any portion of the air you expire during a treadmill run. From this expired air, measurements will be made for oxygen and carbon dioxide, enabling us to determine exactly the amount of oxygen your body utilizes during a run.

Now you're ready for the test. Each one is divided into at least three three-minute runs, which become progressively more difficult. Assuming you're in average condition, we'd set the first run for 5 miles per hour and a 5 percent uphill grade, meaning you would be running five feet uphill for every 100 feet forward. Level running is too easy.

It usually requires three or four technicians to run a test. One technician operates the treadmill and the timer, another directs the expired air into the proper collectors and the third operates the ECG machine. I'm there, too, to observe the electrocardiogram and make any adjustments in procedures to get the data we're after.

Most subjects panic a little at the beginning of a treadmill run and start out with short, choppy steps before settling down to long, graceful strides which adjust more easily to the speed of the treadmill. It makes no difference to your breathing. You start huffing and puffing almost immediately, inhaling room air through a one-way valve, and exhaling expired air into the collecting bags.

After each three-minute run, the treadmill is stopped, and your recovery heart rate is then taken for 15 seconds at one-minute intervals. This still has some importance if it is correlated with all the other information.

Each successive run becomes more difficult since both speed and incline are increased. In addition, you're now running with some built-in fatigue from the first run. When you reach your maximum, your heart rate will peak out at about 180 beats per minute, frequently higher. A well conditioned athlete would reach his maximum at a heart rate of only 170 or 175 beats per minute even though his work load would be considerably greater and his oxygen consumption higher. We've had some highly conditioned men on the treadmill who pushed it nearly to its limits and they still were not exhausted!

It's a real joy to see some of our own subjects, who have taken the treadmill test and subsequently entered an exercise program based on the point system, come back a few months later and take the treadmill test a second time. Their oxygen consumption has gone up and their heart rate has gone down, dramatic proof of one element of the training effect. It's a lovely see-saw to watch.

We measure the oxygen consumption in milliliters (ml) per kilogram of total body weight per minute. It tells us, basically, how much oxygen your body is consuming, canceling out differences resulting from variation in body weight. For example, the 42 ml/min would indicate the same level of fitness in two men even though one weighed 150 pounds and the other 250 pounds. In either case, their bodies would be consuming 42 ml's of oxygen per minute for each kilogram (2.2 pounds) of weight.

The ml figure, as I explained earlier, is the figure we have translated into points. Each exercise requires so many ml's of oxygen to produce the necessary level of work and this is what we have measured. Conversely, the maximum amount of oxygen that your body can process and consume is a measurement of your fitness level, for a conditioned man consumes much more than a deconditioned man.

Let me use some crude examples to illustrate what I mean. The air we inhale contains about 21 percent oxygen. However, during exhausting work, the amount of oxygen exhaled decreases and is a rough indicator of the level of fitness. A deconditioned man may exhale 18 percent oxygen, his body consuming only 3 percent of the oxygen he inhales.

A man in average condition might exhale 17 percent oxygen, his body consuming 4 percent of the oxygen he inhales.

Finally, a conditioned man might exhale only 16 percent oxygen during exhausting work, indicating that his body can consume 5 percent of the oxygen he inhales.

This is all laboratory detail, and significant to a technician, but it shouldn't concern you too much. All you really have to remember is that, as your condition improves, you consume more oxygen and this improvement is measured by the number of ml's you can handle at maximum exertion, and we have translated this into measurable amounts, as points.

Incidentally, in case you're also wondering why we use three-minute runs on the treadmill when I said earlier that five minutes is the break-even point for the training effect, please keep in mind that the treadmill run is a test, not an exercise. The idea is to find out what condition you're in, not get you in condition. We could conceivably do this by running you to exhaustion in one minute. Dash men run themselves to exhaustion in close to nine seconds.

You might also be wondering what the treadmill has to do with you anyway. You'll never get to run on one. Nevertheless it is the most objective and accurate test yet devised for measuring a man's cardiovascular fitness.

But it is terribly time consuming and hardly the ultimate method for testing large groups. It takes four men and an hour to test one man.

I was aware of all this when I started my research. In the first place, our equipment is obviously restricted to Air Force use, and more specifically to research. We can't even let the general Air Force population walk in off the base and use it, let alone the man in the street.

Nor could the average doctor afford to operate one, either in time or money. The cost of the equipment itself is exorbitant, and few doctors can afford the luxury of hiring three more skilled assistants to run it while averaging only one patient per hour.

So this is the dilemma in which I found myself when I began the search for the ultimate man-in-the-street test. I knew we had some of the best testing equipment in the country, but I knew we had to translate its results into terms anyone could use without equipment.

So I did what any researcher does. I began running tests, using myself and some of my troops as test subjects.

We started with the knowledge that the only common denominator between testing a man with equipment and testing him without equipment is the man himself. The idea, then, was to run him on a track to near-exhaustion, then correlate the results somehow with his maximum oxygen consumption on a treadmill.

The best model for this type of test was one developed by my friend and former mentor, Dr. Bruno Balke, formerly with the Federal Aviation Agency and now at the University of Wisconsin. He devised a 15-minute field test, in which the subject would run (or walk) as fast as he could for 15 minutes, and at the end of the exercise, his speed measured in meters per minute would be calculated. This value appeared to correlate well with his maximum oxygen consumption established on a treadmill run.

We made two major revisions in this test to accommodate our peculiar problem of dealing with the mass population of the Air Force. After months of trial and error, varying the times from six minutes up to 20, and taking them back to the treadmill to check them out, we finally settled on 12 minutes as the best time for our purposes. We get excellent results at this level and it allows more tests to be run in a shorter time period.

The second variation was more important. Some of our troops might be hard put to interpret their results, and their condition, in terms of meters-per-minute. We had to find something that would give them the results more rapidly. We ultimately settled on the distance covered in 12 minutes.

That done, the test became, if anything, even more popular

than the point system. Many facilities throughout the country and overseas picked it up as an easily administered field test measuring fitness applicable for individuals and particularly large groups. At this writing, I would estimate that more than 20,000 airmen and officers have used it. And civilians as well.

This always surprises me, because I'm not always sure where the civilians hear about the program. But I often get letters describing the results. One such letter came from a physical educator at a California junior high school. He had been trying the 12-minute test on 13-, 14-, and 15-year-old boys, then comparing it with a 600-yard test—a test used as a standard in some sections of the country—and also with maximum oxygen consumption tests.

He learned three things. The results from two 12-minute tests, run four days apart, were almost identical, indicating a good consistency. The results from the maximum oxygen consumption studies also showed a very good correlation with the 12-minute test, indicating the 12-minute test was a very good substitute for the time-consuming but more accurate oxygen consumption tests. The results from the 600-yard test didn't correlate as well with the oxygen consumption. This indicates to me that it is not as good an indicator of over-all cardiovascular health as the 12-minute test.

Incidentally, 62 percent of those California teenagers made either the good or excellent category on the 12-minute test, a result possibly unmatched by any similar age group outside California. In California they seem to take physical fitness seriously and at an early age too.

So to answer the questions posed earlier, why is the treadmill test important to you? It is important because the 12-minute field test is a method of estimating the maximal oxygen consumption based on laboratory-determined results of treadmill studies. This field test is surprisingly accurate, easy to administer, and it requires no equipment. All that is necessary is a track (or measured distance) and yourself. All you need remember is the time and the distance.

We furnish the time: 12 minutes.

You furnish the distance.

Whatever distance you cover in those 12 minutes can be translated into ml's of oxygen. If you've done the best you can, this figure is your maximum oxygen consumption. It is the same figure, with a small margin of error, that you would get if we had put you on our treadmill and measured your oxygen consumption directly. The margin of error includes such things as wind conditions, temperature—and motivation!

Please keep in mind that it's a *maximum* test. For this reason, I must emphasize the need for medical clearance from your physician before taking the 12-minute test; particularly if you are over 35 years of age.

If you are 35 years of age or under, the initial 12-minute test can be taken without difficulty if you are free from medical problems.

If you are over 35 years of age and *have not been* exercising regularly (at least three times a week for a minimum of six weeks), I would advise against taking the initial 12-minute test. Place yourself in the lowest category of fitness and begin one of the 16-week conditioning programs without testing.

If you are over 35 years of age and *have been* exercising regularly, go ahead and take the 12-minute test.

I will now give you a brief explanation of how to take the 12-minute run/walk test, then give you the chart to check the results.

Find an outdoor or indoor track, or make one of your own up to two miles long. The local high schools usually have a regular quarter-mile oval track and the YMCAs have measured areas inside their gyms. If not, get in your car and, using the odometer, mark off a track of your own in a nearby park or on a lonely stretch of road. It's a one-shot test, so you don't have to get too fancy with it. When you're ready to run, dress comfortably and bring a watch with a sweep-second hand to mark the time exactly. Many men enlist their wives as timers. They follow along in the car, tooting the horn when it's time to start and tooting again to mark the spot where you finish at the end of 12 minutes.

In the Air Force, of course, it is usually done under supervision. The physical training instructor, using a stop watch and whistle, handles large groups en masse. Blowing the start and finish, and having each man check his distance covered (the tracks are usually marked off in tenths of miles), he can handle very large crowds.

Start out running, but, if your breath gets short, walk for a while until it comes back, then run some more. Keep going for the full 12 minutes. When you've checked the distance you've covered in 12 minutes, you can find your oxygen consumption on the chart, and determine your Physical Fitness Category.

Fitness Category	Distance Covered	Oxygen Consumption
I Very Poor	less than 1.0 mile	28.0 ml's or less
II Poor	1.0 to 1.24 miles	28.1 to 34 ml's
III Fair	1.25 to 1.49 miles	34.1 to 42 ml's
IV Good	*1.50 to 1.74 miles	42.1 to 52 ml's
V Excellent	1.75 miles or more	52.1 ml's or more

*For men over 35 years of age, 1.40 miles in 12 minutes is consistent with the good fitness category. For women, the good fitness category appears to be greater than 1.30 miles in 12 minutes. However, our performance studies on women are not yet completed.

If you fall in one of the first three categories, you're not in very good condition. But don't be too discouraged. It's sad but true that about 80 percent of the American population is there, too. In our tests, the first three categories get failing marks. Only categories IV and V are considered passing.

The categories are important because they enable you to determine your current level of fitness and they place you in different conditioning programs. But if you still find the 12-minute run/walk test awkward to run in your area, and would prefer to get right into the conditioning program without it, then drop yourself down to the very poor group and go through the 16-week conditioning course without any testing.

However, the 12-minute test is not only a good measure of fitness, it's an excellent indicator of progress. You can take it again and again during your conditioning program and afterwards, just to see how you improve as you start picking up points and after you top 30.

In fact, I could recommend 12 minutes as a daily exercise program. Check the point charts. See how many points you can pick up in just 12 minutes of running a day. When you get your distance up to 1½ miles in 12 minutes, you can top 30 points in just four days a week—48 minutes of exercise! But before trying any shortcuts, let's get you in shape.

5: The System

THIS CHAPTER is what this book is all about. Anything that went before was persuasion and preparation. Anything that comes after is expansion and documentation.

This chapter is about the point system. It took us four years to develop it; but the point system is really very simple. It's divided into two basic programs: getting you into condition, then keeping you there.

Getting you into condition depends to some extent on the 12-minute test. The test classifies you according to your present condition and tells you exactly how many weeks to spend, and how much exercise to put into each week, to work up to 30 points per week. And once you get there, 30 points per week is what keeps you there.

The test also tells us something about you and how you've been spending your leisure hours lately, in some cases a lot more than you'd really like us to know.

Here are the five categories again. See if you can spot yourself.

CATEGORY I (Very poor). Less than one mile on the 12-minute test, meaning your maximum oxygen consumption is less than 28 ml's/min.

My friend, if you're in this category, you're in desperate need of conditioning. Being unable to run one mile in 12 minutes means your endurance capacity is dangerously low. The maximum amount of oxygen you can utilize during exhausting work is not much more than the amount you use during your normal daily activities.

This category catches all the do-nothings, the desk jockeys, the TV watchers, the over-eaters, the over-smokers, the over-drinkers, the under-workers, the men who would rather ride a block than walk it, and the men who are always complaining, "Doc, who needs endurance?"

And don't plague me with excuses about your health or your age being handicaps. I could shame any one of you with cardiacs who have made magnificent comebacks, and splendid old men who can outperform me even though they're nearly twice my age.

And *they* aren't in this category! If you are, face up to it, you are badly in need of a physical conditioning program. Take the 16-week course, and get active before it's too late. It goes like this:

Weeks	Points/Week
1 thru 3	10
4 thru 6	15
7 thru 9	20
10 thru 12	24
13 and 14	27
15 and 16	30

Take one of the six Category I basic conditioning programs listed on pages 2-7 of the center section or choose your own exercises from the point value charts beginning on page 23 of the center section, or from those in the Appendix.

CATEGORY II (Poor). Less than 1.25 miles and 34 ml's/min.

This category catches the social athlete, the man who plays golf on Saturday, or tennis on Sundays, or baseball at picnics, or goes swimming in summer, or hunting in fall, or skiing in winter—and next to nothing in between.

The shame of this category is that these men are often convinced that this kind of sporadic exercise is keeping them in great shape.

We've had these weekend exercisers on our treadmill and almost without exception, they perform poorly. And they leave our lab convinced that the results must be wrong since the best they could do was 34 ml's/min.

If the best you achieve with weekend golf is Category II, you should change or expand your conditioning program. To

Dear Zhao and He Longjin

Bernice and I hope this book will add years of life in good health for both of you, and your children and patients.

We enjoyed our visit with you, and we are especially interested in your sons — they seem to be quite talented.

Sincerely

Abe and Bernice Fischer

get out of Category II, take one of the six Category II basic conditioning programs listed on pages 8-13 of the center section or choose your own exercises from the point value charts beginning on page 23 of the center section, or from those in the Appendix.

Weeks	Points/Week
1 and 2	10
3 thru 5	15
6 and 7	20
8 and 9	24
10 and 11	27
12 and 13	30

CATEGORY III (Fair). Up to 1.50 miles and 42 ml's/min.

This is the group for which I have the most sympathy. These men try. They're obviously more than weekend athletes, so they're obviously trying to get something extra done in between their days off.

This category usually catches the early morning walkers, the noontime swimmers, the after-work handball or squash players, and all the others who make a conscientious week-by-week, year-round effort to keep themselves in shape.

Gentlemen, I'm genuinely sorry, but whatever you're doing it's not quite enough. If you can't run 1.50 miles, then your maximum oxygen consumption is less than 42 ml's/min and you're a shade short of good condition. And it's probably because whatever regular activity you take, as good as it is, is cut short too soon or is not done often enough to do you the maximum amount of good. It's probably because, as one of the Poopers said earlier, you've never had anything to aim at.

Now, with something to aim at, I hope you can lift yourself that one last notch. Some of you will argue, I'm sure, that you're giving your weekly quota of exercise all the time you can spare, and you just can't spare any more. Well, try walking to pick up those extra points. Many men do.

I remember one distinctly. A desk worker, he swam 20 laps four times weekly. When he came down to our shop to take the 12-minute test, we had him pegged as a 20-point-per-week man and estimated his distance as about 1.4 miles. He astounded us by running 1.63, just short of the excellent category.

When asked if he was holding out on us about his exercise

habits, he said, "No, unless you count the walk between the train and the office."

It turned out they're two miles apart and he walked it twice a day, five days a week, for another 20 points and a 40-point week.

It can be done!

If you want to do it, start with one of the six 10-week Category III training programs listed on pages 14-19 of the center section or develop one of your own from the point value charts beginning on page 23 of the center section, or from those in the Appendix.

Weeks		Points/Week
1		10
2 and	3	15
4 and	5	20
6 and	7	24
8		27
9 and	10	30

CATEGORY IV (Good). More than 1.50 miles and 42 ml's/min.

These are the men who have been earning greater than 30 points a week without ever knowing it, because 30 points and 1.50 miles or more in 12 minutes are consistently compatible.

This category usually catches the same men we met in Category III, conscientious men who push it just a little farther, doing more of the same exercises—swimming, handball, squash or whatever—each day, or spreading them out over more days. Or, what is more likely, they've been picking up some extra points with some extra running, cycling or walking in addition to their competitive activities.

These men aren't in need of a progressive conditioning program. If you're one of them, you can go right on doing what you've been doing, because you must have been doing something right to run 1.5 miles. If you've been doing it without anything to aim at, it might be of some comfort to you now to refer to the point chart and find out how you've been doing it. You might even find better, or quicker, ways of earning the same number of points.

No conditioning program necessary here. Just keep up at least a 30-point week. (Examples of a 30-point week are listed on pages 51 and 52.)

CATEGORY V (Excellent). Better than 1.75 miles and more than 52 ml's/min.

These are the competitive athletes, plus quite a few others who enjoy exercise enough to push themselves harder and maintain their condition at a higher level. I would guess most of them are getting all or most of their exercise from the "big three," running, swimming or cycling. I make Category V easily, and so do many of my Poopers, but we're all runners, earning up to 75 points a week.

This kind of conditioning, however, isn't necessary for the average layman, and that's another advantage of the point system. By giving you a basic minimum to meet—30 points any way you can get them—it lets you set your own maximum. The 30 points will satisfy both your body and your conscience, and keep you comfortably in Category IV.

If you're not satisfied there, then start running and welcome to the club.

Actually, there's a category even beyond V, but the men in this group don't need any help from me. They are the supremely conditioned athletes, amateur or professional, who can consume 70 ml's of oxygen per minute at maximum. The highest consumption rates I've ever heard of were those of some Norwegian cross-country skiers who were tested by my friend and colleague, Dr. Per-Olaf Astrand of Stockholm, Sweden. They topped 80 ml's. Phenomenal! Just imagine, these men at rest don't consume any more oxygen than you and I, yet look what they can do. Their bodies are in such condition that they can increase their resting oxygen consumption as much as 20 times, and then maintain it for long periods. They've been known to maintain heart rates of 170 beats per minute for two and three hours at a time on some of their cross-country treks. Simply phenomenal!

Category V obviously doesn't need any progressive conditioning program either. If you're in it, you're already in condition. Just keep it up.

There is one more category which I call Category X. This is where I put the clinical cases, the cardiacs and others with serious ailments. In the Poopers' Club I can keep my eye on them, and advise them on their rate of progress during the conditioning program. I can hardly do that in a book. Each case is different. Your best advisor is your own doctor. As a rule of thumb, the way it has worked out for most of our clinical cases is to double everything in Category I. (See pages 2-7 of the center section.) Do the first week's schedule for two weeks, the second week's for two weeks, and so on, for a total of 32 weeks of conditioning instead of 16. There is a special program for cardiacs on pages 21-22 of the center section. But you had best set your own pace with your own doctor's guidance.

However, believe me when I tell you that it can be done.

The only inconsistencies we've found in estimating, from their exercise habits, where any man might finish in the 12-minute test are the ex-exercisers and the men who do some form of manual labor.

The ex-exercisers might be men who have been in excellent condition at some time, but then have quit exercising. They start dropping through the categories, from V on down, and the speed at which they drop depends on their initial condition and how fast they begin dissipating. If they take the test at some mid-point in their drop—"What have you been doing lately?" "Nothing!"—it's difficult to predict where they might finish. So the test becomes the best indicator of how far they have fallen, and an excellent goad to get them back on track.

The manual laborers—postmen who walk their routes daily, farmers who haven't become too mechanized, some construction workers, and others who work with their bodies—often do very well, but their activities are hard to measure and it's difficult to estimate what kind of condition they're in.

Again, the test is the best indicator and an excellent yardstick to tell them how many additional points they need, if any, to maintain a 30-point week. Some might get by, for instance, with just 10 points' worth of formal exercise during their off-duty hours.

American farmers have produced some unusual studies. Years ago, you could almost predict, sight unseen, that they were all in excellent condition. Not so today. The farms in some areas have become so mechanized that some of the rural men are not much better off than their sedentary city brothers. The young recruits we get in service today show little difference between boys raised in the city and those brought up on a farm. Sad, but true.

If you found yourself in one of the first three categories, you might want something more than just vague instructions to "go out and get 10 points' worth of exercise the first week" and so on. Actually, I did it this way as an accommodation to those who prefer to go their own route and devise their own conditioning programs. It'll work, because 10 points' worth of exercise will begin to get results regardless of the exercise you choose.

However, for those who want something a little more definite at least for the conditioning period, we've worked out six basic courses based on running, swimming, cycling, walking, running in place and an either/or program of handball/basketball/squash. The last three, we've found, are comparable in their benefits. The charts for all six begin on page 2 of the center section.

The running program, without any equivocation, is the best. It's quick and it's sure—and it's inexpensive. About all you need are comfortable shoes and a place to run. We use it exclusively for newcomers to the Poopers' Club.

I am, of course, fully aware of the medical benefits of running. But beyond this what I like about it most is that I can recommend it to anyone of any age, presuming there is no physical deformity. It exercises the arms as well as the legs, and has a toughening effect on muscle groups throughout the body, notably the abdomen. It is the quickest way to reach a steady state and get that training effect started. Many of the Poopers have taken inches off their waistlines without calisthenics. Running can be done alone or in groups, indoors or out, and at any time of day. And it can be done for the rest of your life—and a long, productive life it should be.

Swimming is a close second, with advantages and disadvantages. The big disadvantage is that some people have an unreasoning fear of water. This can be overcome, of course; but it adds an unwanted handicap when total concentration on conditioning is necessary.

The second disadvantage is that you need a pool, preferably one 25 yards long. However, the YMCAs and commercial health clubs can accommodate most people in urban areas.

The big advantage of swimming is that, for most people, it is much more enjoyable than running. There is a social atmosphere around a pool you won't find on a track at 6 o'clock in the morning.

Swimming has other advantages, too. It's an ageless sport, and it exercises most of the large muscle masses, especially the arms and legs, although not in the same way as running.

You can't expect the same slimming effect from gliding up and down a pool that you get from pounding around a track. But, as with running, it can be done by anyone, alone or in groups, and this flexibility is one of its major virtues.

Cycling is a good match for running and swimming. The obvious disadvantage is that you need a bicycle. Not so obvious is that weather can be a very large factor. I could hardly recommend that anyone cycle on icy streets, and wind conditions can play havoc—and you can't cycle indoors, unless you use a stationary bicycle. The third disadvantage is that cycling doesn't benefit the muscles of the upper body as much as running, and especially, swimming. Most of the power is supplied by the hips and legs, and consequently most of the toughening up goes to these areas.

However I don't consider this a major problem. The aerobic benefits—the training effect—to the internal organs are identical with those of running and swimming. Dr. Paul Dudley White, the noted heart specialist, and others are ardent advocates of cycling. It can be as sociable as swimming; or it can be done alone. When combined with other activities, it can double as transportation, whether riding to work or going on a Sunday picnic.

Europeans, generally, are inveterate cyclists. I could wish there were as many bicycles on our streets as there are on any European road. We might cut down some of that fitness gap between us. The American attitude seems to be, if it moves put an engine on it, whether it's a motorbike or a golf cart.

There are also some stationary bicycles on the market, similar to our bicycle ergometers, which can be of some benefit. I'm speaking of the kind where you furnish the power to pump the pedals, not the kind that is motorized and you just climb on and go along for the ride. The unmotorized kind can be used as a supplement to other outdoor or indoor exercises, or as a backup for those days when you can't get outside to work out.

Walking is the bottom half of running. The running program, in fact, starts out with a few weeks of walking. Some men, however, especially elderly men with ailing or weakened limbs, prefer this less-vigorous method of conditioning. It's quite valid, although, as you can see from the charts, it consumes more time per session.

The overwhelming advantage of walking, however, is that

it can be done by anyone, anytime, anyplace. It doesn't even look like exercise. For those who are timid about being conspicuous, this can be a deciding difference. Also, once you complete your conditioning, it's such an easy way to pick up points. Like that man who walked from the train to the office, it can become part of your daily routine without ever looking like a routine.

Running in place is strictly an indoor exercise—if you're outdoors, why run in one spot? And being indoors is a satisfying advantage for those who are shy about exercising in front of the neighbors. But don't underestimate it. It has all of the advantages of running, except time. It takes longer, but it can be done alone—all alone, with the draperies drawn —and no one will ever know how you suddenly blossomed into condition, bright-eyed and indefatigable.

Running in place also has a secondary advantage. Even if you've chosen running, swimming or cycling as your basic exercise, running in place can easily be substituted for those rainy or cold days when you can't get outdoors or those busy days when you can't get to the swimming pool. You can do it while you're watching the morning news on television, then shower and you're through exercising for the day.

Handball/basketball/squash have the immediately recognizable advantage of competition. Some men crave it. Most of the NASA astronauts, a highly competitive group, are handball players; and the late Gus Grissom was probably the best of the bunch.

However, these three sports eliminate the advantage of conditioning yourself alone, and reintroduce the disadvantage of needing a place to play. Even so, for those who enjoy competition, if only for the sociability of it, any of these three is an excellent way to whip yourself into shape, then keep you there.

With all these basic conditioning courses, please be prepared for sore muscles. Walking and running affect the legs, especially the ankles; swimming, the arms; cycling and running in place, the upper legs; and the competitive sports, the whole body. This muscle soreness is temporary, and only that indicates you're beginning to use muscle groups that have been dormant too long. The Poopers' Club complains most frequently of ankle soreness. If it persists, we just keep them in the early walking program until it wanes, then start them jogging again. But we don't let them quit.

One of the most serious hazards, especially if you have been inactive too long, is to plunge headlong into an exercise program, convinced you can speed up the conditioning process. The Category I running program, for instance, starts with three full weeks of walking. Some men chafe at this, and try to get going faster. We can almost predict that they're going to have trouble, not only with the ankles, but with the joints as well. Some injuries have been so serious that these men had to drop out of the program altogether, eliminating their chances at reconditioning. My best advice is to stick to the charts verbatim. They've been tested and retested, and are safe as well as sure.

Muscle soreness when switching from one exercise to another is also a problem. If you plan switches like this, it's good practice to work into it gradually, starting with very short sessions even while your other exercise program is still in progress. For instance, if you're running outdoors, and plan to switch to stationary running indoors, start a week ahead of the switch with a half minute or a full minute of stationary running, to work the new muscles into shape slowly. Then you'll be ready for the full switch.

The conditioning charts on pages 2-20 of the center section might at first glance seem confusing. Here's how they work.

If you're in Category I, your conditioning program will take 16 weeks. Select one of the six primary conditioning programs listed under this category and follow it daily. Until you have attained a satisfactory level of fitness, it is best to stick with one exercise.

If you're in Category II, your program will require 13 weeks and again you may select any of the progressive programs listed under Category II.

Category III is comparable to the other two except it requires only 10 weeks for completion.

Those individuals who reached Categories IV or V on their initial test, don't need conditioning programs but start right in with a 30-point week. There is one exception and that is with the swimming program. If you reach Category IV or V on the 12-minute test and desire to maintain your fitness by entering a swimming program, this may be rather difficult unless you have been swimming regularly. For this reason, a progressive six-week program is suggested. If you have been swimming to maintain fitness, merely continue following one of the 30-points-per-week swimming programs.

The walking programs for cardiac and clinical patients (see pages 21 and 22 of the center section) need careful study. First of all, they should never be attempted except under medical supervision. They consist entirely of walking. Secondly, a cardiac patient should never train alone. Thirdly, there should be a brief cooling-off period before sitting down to rest or take a shower. The walking pace gets pretty brisk, once you get into it, so cool off with a more leisurely walk back to your car or home. In my research, I rigged it so the cardiac walkers finish their walk at the far end of the track, so they and their escorts can have a slow cooling-off walk back to the laboratory.

Once you've chosen a conditioning program, and completed it, the idea is to stay there. The way to stay there is with a 30-point weekly program. It will keep you comfortably in Category IV or better. If unsure, retake the 12-minute test occasionally.

Neither the 30-point figure, nor the points for the various stages of the conditioning programs, are arbitrary; and they are sound. They are the result of four years of trial and error, and a lot of sweat from a lot of brows. I won't bore you with details of the whole four years, but the highlights can be summarized easily.

First of all, we measured the exercises themselves, then measured how much of them would produce, then maintain, a good training effect.

We measured the exercises two ways, first by oxygen-consumption tests on the treadmill or in the field—by which we determine the kilocalories burned during any given exercise—and second by running track and treadmill tests on men who perform any given sport or exercise regularly.

The treadmill tests for measuring maximum oxygen consumption have been explained. These tests can also be adjusted to measure less than maximum consumption, anywhere from a slow walk to a sprint. And we went up and down the scale with them.

Most of the walking and running measurements were done this way, then correlated with field tests. Other oxygen-consumption tests were done only in the field, because they were obviously impossible on a treadmill. Cycling was one of them. So we rigged a Rube Goldberg attachment to the back of a pickup truck, installed our ECG machine and expired-air collectors on it, then had the subject cycle behind the truck at various speeds and distances. The running in place exercises were measured indoors, but off the treadmill.

With some exercises, the use of equipment was awkward or impossible. Swimming is an example. There's no easy way to chase a man up and down a pool with oxygen-measuring equipment and not affect his performance, with consequently inaccurate data. And I would hesitate to put electrodes for the ECG machine on anyone in a pool full of water. Handball and other competitive sports also would be affected by research equipment. So with these exercises, we relied primarily, in the initial stages, on the kilocalorie charts and oxygen consumption measurements available in the medical literature.

The charts, we found, are not as accurate as our direct measurements of oxygen consumption. This ultimately forced us to draw up our own revised charts with new Calorie-costs for some exercises. Generally, some of these esoteric exercises have been overrated. Golf is a good example. Some researchers, in fact, call it a great way to ruin a good walk. We followed the charts originally, and awarded half a point a hole for golf, or nine points for a round of 18 holes. Later this was reduced to six and finally to three points.

Here's how we made determinations such as this. We put men into exercise programs, using some of these sports like tennis and handball, then ran periodic tests on them; or we tested men who played some of these sports regularly, like golf. These tests proved to be quite adequate, and the oxygen-consumption and energy-requirement data quite realistic.

In any case, after four years of this, we've eliminated most of the doubts. We can almost predict now, just from interviews about his activities, exactly what kind of condition a man is in.

What it all amounts to, then, is that we have accumulated extensive data on the various sports and exercises and their effect on the human body.

That done, we began working out the point system.

It was necessary to establish, first, what level of fitness should be the goal, then establish some easily usable system for reaching and maintaining that goal—the points.

The 12-minute test was a tremendous help in classifying men according to their condition; but it's a maximum test and we needed a more flexible yardstick for the whole of the exercise field. Now in research you start with known facts and work from them toward the unknown. Since I've been a track man all my life, and since I am well aware that distance runners, endurance runners, by any medical standards and at any age level, are consistently among the most fit, I started out using the mile as the basic yardstick, running or walking it at various speeds and correlating it with oxygen consumption.

We found that any man who ran a mile in less than eight minutes six times a week was in Category IV or better and was invariably, as we later worked it out, averaging 30 points a week or more in his exercise program. So 30 points, or its equivalent in exercise, became the goal, and six days of earning five points a day became the basic daily recommendation.

This is the mile chart from which all else grew:

Time (minutes)	Points	Oxygen (ml's/kg/min.)
19:59 to 14:30	1	7
14:29 to 12:00	2	14
11:59 to 10:00	3	21
9:59 to 8:00	4	28
7:59 to 6:30	5	35
under 6:30	6	42

As you can see, a mile run under eight minutes demands an expenditure of 35 ml's of oxygen per minute to produce the required energy. If done daily, six days a week, it produces a beautiful training effect.

So we assigned a mile under eight minutes five points (35 ml's divided by 7) and, from our data, worked up and down the ml-scale in multiples of seven and drew up the chart as you see it. All other exercises, once we had gathered their measurements, were matched against this basic chart. Any exercise that demanded an average oxygen consumption of 35 ml's/kg/min. (or its equivalent in kilocalories) was awarded five points, any that demanded 28 ml's was awarded 4 points, and so on. A 42-ml exercise is twice as demanding as a 21-ml exercise, so the 42-ml exercise gets 6 points, the 21-ml exercise 3 points. This was carried on throughout the entire exercise spectrum.

If all of this sounds unnecessarily complicated, it needn't worry you. You don't have to understand it, just believe it.

I explain it here for the benefit of those men who are intrigued by how such things are worked out and to convince anyone else that the point system was not put together arbitrarily, that it has a definite scientific basis. I can assure you it's the result of long and arduous labor outdoors, and even longer and more arduous bookkeeping indoors.

To sum it up:

• Five points' worth of exercise done daily produces a good training effect.

• Five points should be considered the daily average for a six-day week.

• Any variation in the daily routine is permissible as long as the week averages out to 30 points. Five days at 6 points per day is best. Four days at 7½ points per day is a good "happy medium." Three days at 10 points per day is still of value but you're close to the borderline, because four days of nothing out of 7 is a lot of nothing.

• Any variation from the 30-point week will produce more or less training effect, depending on whether the variation is more or less than 30 points' worth. In other words, 30 points per week will maintain the training effect. More than 30 will increase it. Less than 30, and you start losing it.

Two questions usually arise here. First, if Category IV requires 42 ml's to be considered in good condition on the 12-minute test, why are exercises that require only 35 ml's considered the basic starting point for getting the training effect?

The 12-minute test is a test of your *maximum* oxygen consumption. You don't have to go to maximum to get a training effect. You can pick up a training effect just walking. Look at the mile chart. A 20-minute mile is obviously walking, yet you burn 7 ml's/min and pick up one point. The only hard rule is a 30-point week. The cumulative effect over a week's time keeps your maximum above 42 ml's, the most you could consume at any one time, even though you never come near it during the week. In other words, a 30-point week is equal to a maximum oxygen consumption of 42 ml's is equal to Category IV, is equal to good condition.

Second question, since the points are based directly on the ml's consumed, why not just use the ml-figure and forget about the points?

It's too awkward. It's much easier to keep track of a 30-point week than a 1680-ml week. The figures get out of hand when you deal with larger numbers. It's simple to keep track of a five-point day. You can do it on your fingers. If you're still interested in the medical basis, just remember that one point equals 7 ml's/min. Consume 14 ml's per minute and you earn two points, and so on.

If you now understand how the 30-point week was determined, and you've completed your conditioning, you're on your own. I lay down no hard and fast rules about how to get your 30 points because, as each man has his own poison, so each man has his own antidote.

I could make the same comments I made earlier about the six primary exercises, and recommend any one of them, or a combination of all of them, as the only good way to reach a 30-point week.

But I won't. A conditioning program is one thing, but exercises that a man wants to do for the rest of his life are something altogether different. There has to be some flexibility in it, from day to day, season to season, year to year. Each man has his own problems, and his final solution will be based on how much time he can give exercise, what facilities are available, and his own personal preferences. I can't predict this in every case. In fact, it's one of the reasons for, and one of the major virtues of, the point system. Any man can choose any combination of exercise and, as long as they add up to 30 points, he can be assured he is getting a scientifically measured minimum to keep him active and productive.

To make your choices, turn to the complete point value charts beginning on page 23 of the center section, or to the Appendix.

If you still need some help, I can offer a few sample 30-point weeks.

Exercise	Distance	Time	Frequency	Points	
1. Running	1½ miles	12 minutes	Mon Tues Thurs Fri	7½	
				30	total

This is the quickest way to get 30 points. 48 minutes a week.

2. Walking	1 mile	19 minutes	2X daily 5 days a week	10	
Swimming	40 laps (1000 yards)	30 minutes	Mon Wed Fri	18	
Golf	18 holes		Saturday	3	
				31	total

This is for the downtown executive (and weekend golfer) who works near a swimming pool. He picks up 10 points walking one mile to and from the train station.

3. Walking	1½ miles	29 minutes	2X daily	
			5 days a week	15
Handball/		35 minutes	Mon Wed Fri	15¾
Squash				30¾ total

Another program for the 9-to-5 man near a gym.

4. Stationary running		10 minutes	6X weekly	
				15
Walking	1½ miles	29 minutes	2X daily	
			5 days a week	15
				30 total

This is for the shy ones. No one sees you running in place at home, and walking doesn't look like exercise away from home.

| 5. Cycling | 3 | miles | 11:30 minutes | 2X daily | 30 total |
| | | | | 5 days a week | |

This is for the factory worker who can pedal to and from the plant and park his bike in the parking lot.

All of these programs, and any variations you might devise, can be adjusted to include seasonal sports such as golf, tennis, rowing, skiing and others. But it's almost impossible to put together a 30-point week without including some of the basic exercises, especially walking, or the big three of running, swimming and cycling. You just have to face up to this.

About all that's left in this chapter on the point system is to offer a few words of encouragement, especially during the conditioning program. It can be an agonizing period, trying to turn back the ravages of time and inactivity, and you can easily convince yourself that it's impossible, that the program is too stringent.

I want to convince you of just the opposite, and I have a few thousand case histories to back me up. One comes vividly to mind.

He was a New York writer, a middle-aged desk jockey, a week-end golfer, and not much else. He heard about our program and joined a commercial health club near his office and began swimming.

"I was supposed to do four laps the first week," he told me later. "I tried two the first day and nearly drowned. I wasn't going to settle for that, so I went back the next day and tried three. I nearly collapsed. I had to quit in the middle of the pool and grab onto the side. I inched my way back to shallow water and climbed out exhausted."

It went like that for a month and he more or less abandoned the formal program.

"I didn't quit, but it must have been six weeks before I could even put five laps together nonstop. I'd panic in the middle of the last one, then flail away at the water, convinced I'd never make it to the end. I always did, but I spent the next five minutes sagged over the edge. Sometimes I thought I was going to die right there."

He didn't give up, and sort of reentered the program sideways, progressing very slowly. When he got to the stage where he could put ten laps together without stopping, the training effect finally got to him.

"I found it hard to believe, but, almost overnight, I wasn't tired anymore. My lungs weren't exploding. I did those 10 laps like they were nothing. Next day I tried 12. More nothing. I kept adding two a day—ignoring the program—and soon I was doing 40. It took me nearly six months to put those lousy 10 laps together, then within another month I was doing 40.

"I look back on it now and wonder what all the fuss was about."

I'm convinced this man, if he had stayed with the original program, would have made it anyway. He had a good attitude, and he was in good health otherwise (he held a private pilot's license and took an annual physical), although seriously deconditioned. Part of his problem—and part of the problem with swimming—is that he was not a good swimmer. It takes skill as well as effort. But I'm happy to see them make it any way they can.

My swimming friend has become pretty cocky about it since. "I walk down those crowded New York streets today and sneer at everybody. I look at them and gloat to myself. I'm in better shape than four out of five of you."

It's typical. First agony, then discouragement, then determination, then progress, then success, then smugness.

Try it. Then you, too, can walk down any street and gloat.

6: The Groups

MAJOR JASPER (Jake) LaPresto was sent to me by his physician. Jake was working in a pressure cooker and it was getting to him.

He was involved in designing new wings in an expansion program at a hospital and Jake was going day and night working against some immovable deadlines.

And he had all the classic symptoms of a man walking the plank.

He was overweight, he smoked 2½ packs of cigarettes a day, he was completely inactive, and he was under stress from 7:30 in the morning until midnight, and often on weekends.

First came the ulcer, then gastro-intestinal pains, then they found an abnormality in his colon that needed surgery. But the surgeon refused to operate. He told Jake to lose some weight and build up his cardiovascular reserves which were close to zero. He couldn't take a chance on putting him on the operating table in that condition.

That's when I got him.

Jake was one of the good ones, though. His problems were typical of a busy man who falls into habits of inactivity. But, once he knew what to do, he did it. He began walking the mile, then running it, and went through the whole routine of sore ankles, blisters and calf pains, and "every cigarette I ever smoked came marching by me."

But he lost weight, dropping from 185 to 173, and took

2½ inches off his waistline. "I found I could get by on two meals a day without any discomfort."

He cut down on his smoking. "I was more relaxed. I didn't need them as tension pills."

The fatigue left him. "Seven hours of sleep—good, solid sleep—was enough."

The ulcer symptoms went away. "My mental attitude changed. I could handle the stress better."

And the gastro-intestinal symptoms disappeared. Jake still hasn't gone under surgery and there's a good chance he may never have to.

All in all, Major LaPresto made beautiful progress, but he was still unhappy.

"Ken," he'd say, "look at me. I'm pushing fifty, and you know my medical history. Why should I have to keep up with these young, healthy kids? Why can't you set lower standards for men like me?"

Jake was one of the good ones, but his complaint was not original. I hear it all the time.

"Doc, I'm over two hundred fifty pounds. I can't make thirty points . . ."

"Major, I've been underweight all my life. Shouldn't I have something a little easier . . ."

"But, sir, my legs are short . . ."

"Aw, come on, Ken. I've got eight kids at home. They wear me out. I ought to get twenty points right there . . ."

Everybody's got problems.

Everyone on this earth, it seems, is a special case with a special body that needs a special program. And I'm willing to bet you think you deserve special consideration, too.

My friend, when God made man, He created only two special bodies, male and female. You're either one or the other, and that's as far as your specialness goes.

I don't blame the Jake LaPrestos of this world for requesting special consideration. Each man has his own troubles to cope with, and to him they're genuine. But I do get a little tired, and a little discouraged, when men who ought to know better open up this Pandora's box and offer special concessions arbitrarily, without any medical data to back them up.

So, to answer Jake LaPresto's question, I didn't set the standard of 30 points, nor can I lower it. I just discovered it and passed it on.

I'm not about to say that a man who only gets 29 points a week is physically less fit then one who gets 30, except by that one point's worth. But you could carry that argument all the way down from 29 to zero. What I do say, based on our research, is that 30 points' worth of exercise is the *minimum* that will maintain your body in a condition that we in medicine know to be most consistent with essential health, whether you're 19 or 90.

I'll say further that the 90-year-old should earn at least 30 points and the 19-year-old should earn considerably more.

To put it another way, ask not whether you can do less exercise when you get older, ask instead whether you can do more when you're younger.

I'd like now to go through some of the age groups, and some special groups within those groups, and describe some of our findings with them, plus my recommendations for points-per-week for each. Perhaps you'll find yourself in one of them.

UNDER 18

Obviously, we don't get too many of these youngsters in the service; so my recommendations are based primarily on medical findings by others and on teaching by experts in physical education.

Up to about 10 years of age, highly competitive athletics are not wise. It can have a harmful psychological effect on a child. Unless it's fun, too much regimentation can be traumatic. Most children in this age group can usually find their own forms of activity without competition.

Above 10, however, and especially as he gets into his teens—and more especially as he gets old enough to borrow Dad's car, and starts riding instead of walking—some form of formal exercise should be strongly encouraged, whether he wants it or not. These are very critical years when his young body is filling out, and should be the years when he gets his heart and lungs in shape for their life's work.

It's been well documented in different studies that the young student who gets enough wholesome exercise—and I don't mean he has to have natural ability to be an all-star quarterback, or a high-scoring basketball player; there are plenty of exercises that don't require ability—this type invariably does well in the classroom, too, living up to his full potential as a student. He is more alert, more assertive and more self-confident than one who shuns athletics because of an inferiority complex.

Thirty points is the minimum for this group, but in this age bracket I could recommend as high as 50 a week.

The sad truth is that many young men under 18 aren't even earning 30 points' worth of exercise. How do I know? Because we get them after they're 18, and the American myth of the fitness of our youth is nowhere more evident than it is on the days when we put new recruits through their first 12-minute test. Nearly two-thirds of them fail to make it into the good category, and these boys are barely out of their teens. Passive fitness, yes, or they wouldn't have been accepted for service, but good condition, no.

The saddest part of this truth is that young men like these, the kind that have had little or no history of activity—and, in many cases, I mean no activity of *any* kind—are imbued with this do-nothing attitude for the rest of their lives, and it becomes almost impossible to shake them out of their lethargy.

And the average age of the American male who succumbs to a heart attack keeps sliding lower and lower. It's something for parents and educators to think about.

FROM 18 TO 50

This constitutes the great bulk of the Air Force population, and consequently the great bulk of my research subjects. We don't get many before the age of 18, and they start retiring after 50. So most of my data is based on this age group.

The recommendation here is a definite 30-point minimum for all of them, with considerably more for some of them, as I shall explain.

I'd like first to go back to those recruits and tell you what happened to them. As I said, nearly two-thirds of them, about 65 percent—and all in their late teens and early 20s—finished their 12-minute tests in one of the first three categories, very poor, poor, and fair. Just six weeks later, however, after completing their conditioning programs, more than 90 percent made Category IV or V, leaving less than 10 percent behind them.

In similar tests at the Squadron Officers' School (SOS), mentioned earlier, and at the Air Command and Staff College (ACSC), we had similar results at the end of conditioning programs. What I found more significant, and more frightening, was that in the initial 12-minute test, as we went from the teenage recruits to a 28-year average age at SOS and a 34-year age at ACSC, the percentage of men in poor condition grew with age.

If the trend is like this in any military service where there are compulsory physical fitness levels to meet annually, what can it be like in civilian life where there are no mandates or "orders from above" to stay in condition? What happens especially to those teen-agers who don't exercise, who don't get into the service where rigid discipline exists, and who go right on doing nothing the rest of their lives? How long are those lives, and what kind of lives are they?

I'm told that middle age in the average American male now begins at 28, that the seeds of heart disease, lung ailments, ulcers, diabetes and the whole gamut of cripplers have already been sown.

But, cheer up! As I said, all of these groups that we tested improved remarkably after completing their conditioning course. The most remarkable improvement of all was noted in my own Poopers' Club. More than 60 percent—that's right—finished, not merely in Category IV, but in Category V, topping 1.75 miles in 12 minutes. The average age is 28, but some of them, like Jake LaPresto, push 50.

Here are a few random samples.

Major Philip Taylor, 38, my assistant director and administrative officer, was a typical over-35 type who had started deconditioning. A high-school football player, he just fell into the "habit of inactivity." He got listless just sitting at his desk all day, then went home and tossed and turned most of the night. Once he started running, however, his latent athletic instincts blossomed again to the extent that he was running up to five miles a day and earning 60 points a week. He, too, pulled his belt in a few notches, and now sleeps "twice as long and twice as hard."

Carlyle Lutz, 47, a civilian psychologist who was invited over by a military friend, was a do-it-yourself calisthenics enthusiast—"I always thought that was the thing to do"—but he became intrigued by the progressive endurance goals of the Poopers' Club. He now runs 1½ miles daily, and admits, "I've toughened up more by running than when I was doing my situps. In fact, I can do more situps now."

Major Paul Hibberd, 49, associate chief of pharmacy for the Air Force, stationed at Wilford Hall Hospital, by his own admission "smoked like a fiend." Curiosity brought him over when we sent out one of our periodic calls for volunteers for the treadmill. He was fatigued within five minutes and went home and brooded. He was back within a week and started running around the track. It took him six months, but he finally broke an eight-minute mile, and on some days he now runs 10 miles. Paul placed third in a local 10-mile marathon race sponsored by the YMCA, and he is one of the founders, without any help from me, of a Century Club among the Poopers, men who earn 100 or more points every week.

More important, after averaging two packs of cigarettes a day for more than 20 years, Paul quit cold—"I just lost the taste for them."

But he gained something else. He became one of the most garrulous of the Poopers, and a one-man proselytizer for an unofficial Cigarettes Anonymous. He bends a lot of ears, including mine, talking about his victory, and more than one man joined the club, at his suggestion, just to find a way to quit smoking.

One of the most unusual members of the club is the pastor of my church, Dr. Buckner Fanning. The church has more than four thousand members, so I was surprised he knew about my work. But he called me one day. "Ken, you might have something I need."

Dr. Fanning went on to say that he had the typical pressures and responsibilities of the twentieth-century church—plus speaking, writing, counseling, and traveling a great deal. With the exception of playing golf, he assumed he could not take time out for serious physical conditioning. He said, "I had a feeling that I needed to do something about physical fitness, but I didn't know where to begin."

The results were typical, too, of a busy man. "I began running out of energy in the middle of the afternoon. Some days, just when I needed to be at my best, I felt like I had to push to get everything done."

I invited Dr. Fanning out to our laboratory and ran both a 12-minute and a treadmill test on him, and found he qualified for Category III, which is not too bad for a 41-year-old man who is not actively involved in a physical-fitness program. Within ten weeks, just like the textbook says, he was running daily, doing a mile and a half in less than twelve minutes. And his energy reserves are now way up.

Dr. Fanning quipped, "I followed the program religiously and it has made a tremendous difference in my life and work. I am continuing active participation in the program and encouraging others to get started. It really works!"

Then there were some others, like Major LaPresto, with clinical conditions.

Airman Ronald Powlas, a personnel specialist at nearby Kelly Air Force Base, and Capt. Rondald Parker, a command pilot with more than 4200 hours in the air, both developed adult onset diabetes.

Powlas, 25 and 20 pounds' overweight, was caught during a routine physical. The doctor who found the sugar told him about our program, explaining, "Fat can't handle sugar very well. You can help relieve the problem by exchanging some of the fat for lean muscle."

"I was skeptical," Powlas says today, "but, when I came over here and saw the others running, I figured, 'Why not?'"

Within eight weeks he was running up to 1½ miles a day. He didn't lose any weight, at our request (which I'll explain in a moment), but he did indeed change fat to lean, losing two inches off his waist in two months. All his sugar tests have subsequently been negative.

Captain Parker was one of the sad ones. A pilot most of his life—he was flying the huge 200-passenger C-124 *Globemaster* troop transport when they discovered the sugar during his annual physical—he was grounded on the spot. After 4200 hours in the air, and just 36 years of age, he had to be removed from flying status.

His was a classic case, however, both causes and symptoms. He sat all day—"either at a desk or in the cockpit"—he was about 20 pounds' overweight, smoked a pack and a half a day, and his family had a positive history of diabetes.

Also, "I was tired all the time, urinating excessively, and constantly thirsty." A typical diabetic!

So he began running, and it took some perseverance. Sedentary too long, his ankles became extremely painful, one of the worst cases I'd ever seen, and he had to drop back to walking on several occasions. But he didn't quit.

Eventually he ran a mile in 7:30 and 1.5 miles in 12 minutes. But, more important, he lost four inches off his waist, going from 38 to 34, and converting 25 pounds of fat to muscle!

Powlas and Parker both agreed to a special program, by which they would not lose weight as recorded on a scale. But they both lost fat! This was an attempt on my part to show that the high blood sugar seen in over-weight diabetic subjects could be controlled by changing fat tissue to lean tissue. We measured the change in a special "Archimedes tank" which measures the total body volume. The subject is submerged in a special water tank, and the amount of water displaced tells us the body volume. This is compared with the total weight, and the relationship of fat weight to lean weight can be deduced by formula.

The program worked for both Powlas and Parker, especially Parker. Within 15 weeks his condition had improved to the extent that his return to flying status is being considered.

Major Robert (Rusty) Cortner is one of our stars.

Rusty, 42, chief of professional education at Wilford Hall Hospital, had ulcer symptoms, was about 25 pounds overweight, and was taking shots for tendonitis. And his back ached, not uncommon for a short man supporting a large front.

Rusty began running, suffering through the ankle pains, got his mile down below eight minutes, then began adding miles and subtracting weight and ailments. Soon he was up to five miles a day and down to 150 pounds from 175. "I found I could get by on two meals of food and five miles of track," he quips.

His ulcer symptoms have disappeared, the shots have been stopped, and his back is painless. Plus the fact that Rusty is one of the few Poopers who actually seems to enjoy his running for its own sake—all five miles of it—and talking about it afterward. On numerous occasions we've discussed his response to the training program and since he holds a doctor's degree in psychology his comments have been very valuable.

"Physically, the changes are obvious," he says. "Take the

ulcer. I love Mexican food (the San Antonio area probably has the finest Mexican food outside of Mexico), but I didn't dare go near it. Now I can eat it seven days a week if I want."

He goes on. "But that isn't it. The change in attitude is the big change. Even at work. I've got a frustrating job, but now I love it. I've learned to relax. I can accomplish so much more, get so much more done without worry or fatigue, that work has become a pleasure.

"Exercise isn't just for the physically unfit. It's for the mentally unfit, too. I can recommend it for anyone who's depressed."

Rusty, incidentally, won the over-40 category of that YMCA marathon mentioned earlier.

Then we had some heart cases.

Captain James Youngson, 29, was told he had rheumatic heart disease, a heart disease usually associated with rheumatic fever in childhood. He was refused insurance and told not to exercise excessively. But, when he heard one of my lectures at SOS, he looked me up when he returned to the San Antonio area.

He entered the program with a vengeance, working up to 30 points in 12 weeks, exercising five times weekly, and making excellent improvement otherwise. His heart rate and blood pressure have come down, and his endurance has gone up, from 1.15 miles in the 12-minute test to 1.65 miles.

Sergeant Roy Hughes, 32, had a congenital heart defect that required open heart surgery. We got him after surgery. The operation was successful, but his recovery was not. He became fatigued just sitting, and generally deteriorated after his operation. So rest after surgery was not the answer.

Another one of our subjects, age 42, was a cardiac case. He'd been hospitalized for chest pains, then discharged. Two weeks later he had a heart attack. He recovered from it but the chest pains became constant, recurring daily for 3½ months before he was finally sent to us. By then he was taking nitroglycerin tablets every day to relieve the pain.

Within a week after he started walking, following the cardiac conditioning program, the pains began to disappear and he reduced his medication.

However, six weeks later he had a relapse. When the cardiac chart got him up to 1½ miles a day, one day he became dizzy and the pain came back when he sat down after his workout. I don't think it was the distance as much as the fact that he sat right down after his walk. Since then, as I mentioned earlier, we've had all the cardiacs finish at the far end of the track so that they can have a "cooling off" walk back to the shop.

Even so, it's another indication that men with clinical conditions should not be forced to follow the charts rigidly, but should be brought along progressively on an individual basis under strict medical supervision. Some of them will require up to a year to finish their progressive conditioning program.

Chief Master Sergeant Robert Hill, 44, noncommissioned officer in charge (NCOIC) of dental services at Wilford Hall Hospital, had a heart irregularity—an arrhythmia that jumped his resting heart rate as high as 180 beats per minute about once a month. He was also overweight.

Sergeant Hill began walking, then running, and within a few months was well below eight minutes for the mile, and running up to 20 miles a week. His arrhythmia now recurs only once every four or five months. He is a walking testimonial for the benefits of this program.

Cooper's Poopers' Club followed the point system rigidly. Exceptions were the clinical cases and those with severe ankle pains who were allowed to stretch the conditioning periods. Once they worked their way up to Category IV and 30 points a week, however, they were required to stay there.

Some of them, more than 60 percent of them, went beyond this, earning up to 100 points a week and moving into Category V. The reports from all the other bases using the system parallel what we learned here at Wilford Hall Hospital.

So I don't have to apologize for the 30 points. It is defensible in the laboratory and provable in the field.

The results speak for themselves. The subjects bracket the whole age group from raw 18-year-old recruits to veterans pushing 50, and they touch most bases on the medical spectrum, from simple deconditioning to serious cardiac conditions. All who persevered worked their way back to Category IV or better; and all are maintaining more than 30 points a week and enjoying good health.

More than that, it's changed their lives. You've had some of their reactions, and you'll get more when we get into the training effect and the clinical conditions. Most of the Poopers, when you ask them, will give almost the same answers to the same questions, that they sleep better, that they can work longer with less fatigue, that they're more relaxed, and so on. Senior Master Sergeant Boyd Smith, 42 (NCOIC of anaesthesiology service), had one answer that was different. He said, "I find I can get up out of a chair faster."

It's not a big thing, but it shows the thoughts that occupy a man's mind when he begins worrying about his health, and his feeling when he improves it. For Sergeant Smith, it was getting up out of a chair faster. For you, it might be something else just as trivial and every bit as important.

The 18-to-50 group, as I said, should maintain a minimum of 30 points per week. A few special groups should get even more. Here are some of them:

The Fat Boys' Club. What you are about to read should make you wince.

All of the military services get a small percentage of recruits that, to put it mildly, are grossly overweight. So much so that they can't possibly participate in the ordinary routine of basic training. What can be done with them?

I'll tell you what the Air Force does with its "baby whales" (as the boys call themselves).

They're put in a special group with a special program that goes something like this. The bugler blows them out of bed at 5 A.M., and they've got one hour to prepare for inspection. At 6 o'clock they fall out—for breakfast? Nonsense, they run four laps around the drill field.

It kills their mammoth appetites somewhat, and it's just as well. Breakfast usually consists of something like a small dish of fresh fruit, two poached eggs on dry toast, and coffee.

They get one hour of ground school, then from about 8 o'clock until noon it's four solid hours of exercise, starting with 15 minutes of calisthenics, then a mile-and-a-half march to the gymnasium where they run more laps, work out on weights and pulleys, play competitive sports, and finish off with more calisthenics. Then another 1½-mile march to the dining hall.

After a light lunch, they're ready—for bed? Again nonsense. They're thrown into another 2½ hours of exercise, including more running and marching. And they don't have any more to look forward to at dinner than they had at lunch. They're in bed—and glad of it—by 8 o'clock.

In a normal 24-hour day, these "baby whales" get 6½ hours of exercise, including up to eight miles of running, nine hours of sleep, and only 2½ hours of free time during which they clean up their barracks and take care of their personal hygiene. Their total food intake daily averages about 1100 Calories, about what you and I frequently consume in one meal.

But it works.

Each of them loses enormous amounts of weight, but the significant loss is in fat weight. One of the best examples lost only 12 pounds of total weight, but 25 pounds of fat. He had converted the other 13 pounds to lean muscle.

So next time you're feeling sorry for yourself trying to keep up a 30-point week, remember the "baby whales" and their 6½ hours of exercise and 1100 Calories of food.

Athletes. Amateur and professional athletes are at the opposite end of the scale from the "baby whales." They push themselves voluntarily well beyond the 30-point level, and in recent years they've obviously been pushing themselves harder than ever.

Dream track records, once thought impossible, have been broken with abandon. The four-minute mile is now routine, the 17-foot pole vault is common, the 70-foot shot-put mark has fallen, the 200-foot discus throw is long gone, and the 7-foot high jump has been scaled. Where will it end?

Several studies have been made in this area, searching for reasons. Food has been found mostly irrelevant; any well-balanced diet is sufficient for peak performance. Equipment, notably fiber glass poles, has had some effect, but still does not account for the number of athletes breaking formerly "insurmountable" records. Drugs have been under sporadic suspicion, unnecessarily, because tests prove that, apart from their harmful side effects, drugs actually restrict top achievement.

The only common denominator researchers could find was the difference in recent training methods over those used decades ago when some of the dream records were only wishful thinking. The more vigorous endurance conditioning, the kind that builds up cardiovascular reserves, is given most of the credit for the recent rash of record breaking.

Endurance training produces more potential energy, because the body is equipped to push more oxygen around when needed, and for longer periods of time without fatigue. Consequently, the athlete has more reserves available not only during an event, but between events as well. He can use these reserves to practice his specialty much longer without tiring, spending more time perfecting his technique.

So endurance training can be recommended for any sport, even if the sport itself doesn't require endurance.

I once read where the great Ty Cobb boasted that he got himself in shape for the baseball season in spring training, then coasted the rest of the year. "Let the other guys knock themselves out," he'd rasp.

Knowing Cobb's combative approach to the game, I suspect he was trying to psyche his competitors. Baseball has often been called "the long season," and if his competitors took his advice—i.e., "goofed off" as he claimed he did—they'd run out of steam toward the end of the season while Ty, who kept himself in shape all year round, was still going strong.

George Halas, the owner-coach of the Chicago Bears professional football team, allegedly would fine his players if they showed up at summer camp overweight, and he'd keep the fine up daily until they got down to playing weight. "They're grown men," he'd snarl, "I'm not going to baby them." Obviously, George was another firm believer in year-round conditioning.

That's my second piece of advice for athletes. In addition to endurance training, regardless of your specialty, keep yourself in shape all year round. The end of any season, or any event like the fourth quarter in football, can get to an athlete who has allowed his reserves to dwindle and then tries to build them up again just before a season or an event. You'll be lucky if you get them high enough, and you'll waste valuable time trying, time that could have been spent practicing technique or getting individual muscles in condition.

I would recommend a bare minimum of 50 points per week during the off season for anyone who is serious about athletics, and for those involved in endurance sports, such as basketball, soccer or boxing, the minimum should be as high as 100.

Endurance runners, those involved in races where endurance itself can be the deciding factor, should get up to 500 points a week. Most of the great distance runners, from Emil

Zatopek, through Peter Snell and Jim Ryun, ran 100 miles a week or more, and not all of it on flat surfaces.

Think of these men when you're complaining about your mere 30 points per week.

There is one more thing to do before leaving the subject of athletes, and that's to clear up the two most persistent myths about them; i.e., that an "athlete's heart" is something to be avoided, and that anyone who "burns out" his body when he's young doesn't have anything left for middle age or old age.

I'll go into more detail on the heart in the next chapter, but let me say here that several studies have exposed both these views as nonsense.

First of all, the athlete's heart, if different from normal, is definitely above normal. The heart is a muscle and, like any muscle that is exercised intelligently, grows stronger with use. Many athletes have hearts that are larger than normal —more muscular, if you will—and consequently stronger and more efficient.

What confuses people is that when some friend or relative dies, and the cause of death is discussed, someone might confide that the doctor said "his heart was enlarged." Some sick hearts *are* enlarged, but this is by no means an "athlete's heart." A diseased heart can enlarge the same way any diseased muscle might swell up, but there is certainly no corresponding increase in strength and efficiency. Just the reverse. You might think of an athlete's heart as a muscular, healthy heart, and an enlarged heart as a swollen, unhealthy heart.

The second myth, that an athlete cuts down his life span by "burning up" his body too soon, has no medical foundation. Some athletes do die young, and they get a lot of publicity when they do, but a good many more die old, and all they rate is a small obituary buried in the back pages, probably because there aren't enough of their contemporaries around for their deaths to rate better space.

Comparative studies have been done in this area, some going back to the last century, and all prove that athletes generally live at least as long as their contemporaries and, in many cases, years longer. What's more significant, however, is what kind of years they are, healthy or unhealthy? An athlete who finishes his career, then quits exercising altogether, is not much better off in the fight for survival than a nonathlete who has never exercised at all. I suspect that the myth about "burning up" *young* grew from just such athletes, those who trained twice as hard during their careers then dissipated twice as much when they finally broke loose from their Spartan routine. More than one two-fisted fighter ended up as a two-fisted drinker.

The myths laid to rest, I can recommend competitive athletics to anyone who has the physical talent to participate. It's an old cliché, but competition on the track or on a ball field does much to prepare a young man for the competition of life itself. There is a lot of evidence to support the proposition that a man successful on the field is likely to be successful in life.

I would only warn that, once the competition has ended, the physical activity should not end with it.

Aviators. Reading aircraft accident reports is one of the unpleasant duties of a flight surgeon, but often the behavior of the aircrew under stress puts a rosy glow on the world again.

One of my favorite stories involves a multi-place jet bomber on a routine flight. Nearing 30,000 feet, with the cabin pressurized at 9000 feet (simulating the atmosphere found at that altitude), the plexiglass canopy over one of the crewmen burst. This caused a rapid decompression in the cockpit, meaning that the cabin altitude changed instantly from the relatively dense atmosphere of 9000 feet to the thin air of 30,000 feet, the actual altitude of the aircraft. Worse, one of the crewmen, because of his duties at the moment, was not strapped in and was torn loose from his oxygen supply and sucked through the hole in the canopy, his feet miraculously catching the instrument panel. So he was dangling half in and half out of the aircraft, in the harsh rush of air near the speed of sound, in the freezing temperatures of 30,000 feet, and without oxygen.

While the pilot initiated emergency procedures to slow the aircraft down and return to lower altitudes, the other two crewmen unstrapped themselves and grappled with their colleague to haul him back in. Then, alternately using their own masks, they fed him oxygen. He was unconscious by now, but still alive.

The aircraft returned to base and the stricken crewman was rushed to the hospital. It was five hours before he regained full consciousness, yet neither he nor the other three crewmen suffered any lasting effects from their story-book flight, except for some temporary pain when their ears popped from the rapid decompression.

The accident report concluded, "His excellent physical condition without a doubt was a big plus in this crewman's recovery."

I say, "Amen" to that, and add that the other three men must also have been in better-than-average condition to handle not only the physical stress involved, but the emotional strain of saving a stricken colleague under hazardous conditions and getting their crippled aircraft back to safety.

Physical and emotional stress, if a problem for the average man, is much more so for the modern military pilot. The complexities of supersonic aircraft and the stresses of long subsonic and supersonic flights, are very demanding on the men who fly them.

And sometimes these men need help in meeting that demand.

Aerospace medicine is another of my specialties. Therefore, our whole research program—and this book—ultimately grew out of the need to help aviators and astronauts be better prepared physically to meet the demands of flight.

Ordinarily you'd think pilots would keep themselves in top physical condition. A lot of them do but others are not so well motivated. Since Air Force pilots are intelligent men— their average IQ is around 120—they know the importance of keeping themselves physically fit.

One doctor who tried to formulate a special program for a group of pilots stopped short of getting too specific about it. "Attempts at individual improvement," he reported, soberly, "are often resented as attacks on self-sufficiency."

But, when they show up at my office on those lonely mornings, their track shoes under their arms, and everything but hope gone, their self-sufficiency is somewhat shaken. I wish on those mornings that I could have reached them sooner.

I tried once, early in our program, when I printed an article in an Air Force publication, *Aerospace Safety*. It was the first time the point system had ever been mentioned in print, and it drew a tremendous response. This was something a self-sufficient pilot could understand, just give him a goal to reach and let him reach it by means of his own choosing. I called the article "Flying Status Insurance"—the insurance, of course, being the preventive medicine of aerobic exercise.

I realize there are only a limited number of pilots around but, when I use this material in my lectures, even laymen find the glamor of the pilots and their problems the most interesting part of the program.

I would like now to describe some of these problems and explain how "flight insurance" can help solve them.

Modern aircraft, especially high-performance supersonic jets, represent an incredible advancement in the state of the art when compared to what the Wright brothers started out in, and even to the superb fighting machines of World War II. It almost takes a college education just to understand their electronics and aero-dynamics, let alone climb in and fly one. But there's always a waiting list of highly motivated men who are anxious to try.

What then can aerobic exercise do for them, when all they do is sit? In the first place, the increased performance, increased speed, increased range, and increased complexity of these aircraft can only increase the fatigue of the men who must understand and fly them, sitting or not. Crewmen with larger energy reserves can resist this strain for longer periods of time, and bounce back more quickly when it finally does start affecting them. Also, because of the increased educational and training requirements and the tendency to keep men flying longer, the average age of the trained pilot is rising. It's no longer just a young man's game; and the problems of fighting fatigue are more acute than ever.

The other side of the coin of fatigue is alertness. Those with a high level of fitness invariably have a quicker reaction time than deconditioned men. Studies, on both automobile drivers and aviators, prove it. A fatigued person tends to accept lower standards, makes more errors and reacts to emergencies more slowly. And emergencies in high-performance aircraft can be very "unforgiving," as they say in the trade. The accident reports prove it.

The next problem is G-tolerance. I'm sure you're all familiar with G-forces, from the blast-offs at Cape Kennedy, if nothing else. The force of gravity (G) is multiplied from pressures such as this. For military pilots, the G-forces build up each time they make a tight turn or pull up in a steep climb, and the faster the plane the faster the Gs build up. The body is going one way but the blood wants to go another way, all the way down to the ankles.

Studies correlating physical fitness with G-tolerance show that up to about four or five Gs there's not much difference, but after that conditioned bodies can tolerate the stress better. What happens is that, as the blood pools in the legs, it deprives the brain of oxygen and the pilot "blacks out." Again, as they say down on the flight line, it's "non-habit forming." A conditioned body, however, has the ability to strain against this pooling and force the blood back to the heart where it can be pumped up to the brain.

Those four men in the jet encountered two more of the hazards peculiar to aerospace work, hypoxia and rapid decompression. Hypoxia rapidly produces an oxygen debt. Athletes incur it by performing exercises so vigorous that the body can't bring in enough oxygen to produce the needed energy. Pilots incur it by exposure to altitudes where the pressure of oxygen is insufficient to meet the needs of the body.

This is exactly what happened to the crewman in the jet. What takes place in the body at a time like this, and what does good condition have to do with it? It has to do with the training effect. A man in good condition has the physical capacity to resist the loss of normal oxygen supplies for longer periods and to transport more oxygen, more quickly, to the body tissue when it becomes available again.

This has been tested in pressure chambers. At simulated high altitudes an endurance-trained man can maintain useful consciousness much longer than a deconditioned man. When the oxygen supply dwindles, or is cut off, the body tissue becomes starved for oxygen and the brain tissue is most sensitive to this starvation, so unconsciousness occurs within minutes. But a well-conditioned man, who has more efficient heart and lungs, a larger blood volume, and more blood vessels saturating the various body tissues, can better tolerate a high altitude or low oxygen stress. When the oxygen supply is restored, the process is reversed and he is quicker to recover. If the same man were in poor condition in similar circumstances, the difference in time between losing consciousness and regaining it, might mean permanent damage to the brain or even death.

The second problem, rapid decompression, may result in

the "bends." These bends are caused by nitrogen stored in the body which, at the low pressure of high altitude, bleed off and accumulate around joints. If the decompression is gradual, moving from the normal pressure of sea level to the low pressures of altitude, the body can usually handle it. However, if the decompression is sudden, as in the jet accident, the rapid bleeding off causes the nitrogen to form bubbles. As these bubbles accumulate in or around joints, the pain can be excruciating, even incapacitating. If the bubbles enter the blood stream and reach the brain, they could be fatal.

This danger exists each time a pilot goes to high altitude. Here again condition plays a role. Nitrogen, which is 79 percent of the air we breathe, is not used in the body but some of it is absorbed quite readily in fat tissue. And the more fat tissue a pilot has, the more storage capability he has for nitrogen and consequently the more susceptible he is to the bends.

Modern life-support equipment helps eliminate part of this problem. Most high-performance aircraft carry 100 percent oxygen. If the pilot breathes pure oxygen prior to a high altitude flight, he eliminates a lot of the nitrogen stored in his body. The lean, well conditioned pilot has an advantage over his obese colleague because his tissues are better supplied with blood vessels. Consequently he can eliminate nitrogen more rapidly. On the contrary, the obese pilot carries most of his nitrogen with him where, in an emergency, it could be a serious hazard.

There is one more very large element of danger that confronts today's Air Force pilots and crewmen in the line of duty. Accidents happen, emergencies arise. But suppose the pilot or crewman survives the emergency, what then? You have to appreciate the international scope of Air Force commitments today to understand this problem. The Air Force understands it and maintains schools in remote areas to teach its air crewmen how to survive if they are forced to bail out over an ocean, over a South American jungle, over a North African desert, even over the Arctic ice wastes.

The techniques of survival in these schools are taught in a week. Conditioning is not. There is more than one case on record of a man bailing out successfully, doing everything he should, only to succumb to the elements because his body was too weak to tolerate them.

The final danger to a pilot has nothing to do with the hazards of his duties. It has to do with whether he'll be allowed to perform his duties at all. In my experience as a flight surgeon, the major causes for grounding a pilot or crewman, often permanently, involve heart disease, high blood pressure, duodenal ulcers, glaucoma, diabetes, and obesity. Each of these conditions seems to be more prevalent in deconditioned crewmen, and some of them respond quite nicely to a conditioning program.

Pilots and crewmen are above-average individuals and should keep their bodies in above-average condition. I recommend 30 points per week minimum for all of them, and 40 to 50 if they're in high-performance aircraft.

Astronauts. If conditioning is important to an aviator, it is even more important for an astronaut. The problems are magnified enormously.

The spacecraft are much more complex.

The flights are many times longer, counted in days instead of hours.

And the realm in which the astronauts travel is a void, empty of everything, including atmosphere, pressure and oxygen.

So an astronaut's condition must be even better than his terrestrial counterpart's.

His resistance to fatigue must be high, if only because of the duration of the flights.

His reaction time must be instantaneous, because split-second decisions might mean the difference between survival and disaster.

His tolerance of G-forces must be greater, because the lift-offs and reentries sometimes reach 10 and 12 Gs.

His potential problems of hypoxia and rapid decompression are many times more severe because of the vacuum of space. His problem of survival in extreme environments, if brought down off course, must be considered constantly.

There is one more problem, however, that is peculiar to astronauts alone—weightlessness.

The astronauts have said, without exception, that the feeling of weightlessness itself is really a very pleasant sensation. It's what weightlessness does to them that causes the problem.

On earth, all of us, whatever work we do, have to work

against gravity. Just lifting your arm requires energy to over-come the force of gravity. Remove this force, and most movements become effortless. Add to this the confinement of the spacecraft, where hardly any movement is possible, and you have set the scene for deterioration of the body. Effortless movement and no movement at all means the body is not getting much beneficial exercise, and deterioration on space flights to date shows that the body deconditions at a far more rapid rate than is generally realized. As the flights get longer, the deterioration could become a matter of utmost concern.

We've proved some of this in space-simulating bed-rest studies at Wilford Hall Hospital. Keeping subjects in bed for up to 20 days to simulate the inactivity of weightlessness, we showed that the bones lose calcium, the muscles lose tone, and the cardiovascular system weakens, all serious trends when the astronauts still have to suffer the stresses of re-entry.

Calcium is excreted, via the kidneys, through the urine. If the excretion is too large it could form stones that could lodge in the narrow tube between the kidney and the bladder, an extremely painful condition. And the loss of calcium is directly related to the length of the flight.

The muscles atrophy (waste away) from prolonged inac-tivity, and some muscle tissue may even turn to fat. Any ath-lete who stops training will not deny it, and any patient who has ever spent long periods in bed or had a limb in a cast will confirm it. The muscles need exercise to stay lean and hard.

Perhaps the most serious problem, however, is what hap-pens to the heart and blood system, and it's just the opposite of the training effect. Because of the weightlessness and inac-tivity, the heart doesn't have to work as hard any more, so it grows smaller and beats faster. There is a loss of blood volume and of red blood cells, and the blood vessels lose their tone because of reduced use.

However, all this might be relatively innocuous, if the as-tronaut never had to leave his cushioned space seat. But fa-tigue is necessarily creeping up on him, alertness is dwindling, the G-forces of reentry are still ahead of him, and the dangers of emergencies are all around him. He must face them all with a deteriorating body.

He must also do something else. When the astronauts began taking space walks out of the spacecraft and performing work preliminary to the work involved in landing on the moon, it was observed that extra-vehicular activity (EVA) took a lot more out of them than anyone had anticipated. One of the astronauts ran a heart rate up to 170 beats per minute during his seemingly simple extra-vehicular activities, and the EVAs of other space walkers showed similar findings. The unforeseen work load of space-walking was solved only by a series of hand holds on the spacecraft and by a system of "window washer" strap-ons so the astronaut wouldn't float away from the vehicle and then have to fight his way back. However, interposing frequent rest periods, averaging about two minutes every 10 minutes, was the most effective way to reduce the physical stress of extra-vehicular activity.

What must be done, as space flights continue to grow in complexity and length, is to get the astronauts in top condition before they leave for space and, especially, keep them in good condition while they stay in space.

Keeping the astronauts fit on the ground hasn't been much of a problem. The openings are few and the candidates are many; and even for those who are accepted the flights are infrequent and the competition is keen. They *know* they have to stay in condition just to get an assignment. The test pilots who won slots had some background in physical conditioning; but it was rough on some of the nonpilot scientists who had been bookworms most of their lives. They had some agonizing readjustments to make.

The NASA astronauts follow no rigid exercise program—they're former military pilots mostly, and like most pilots they resent any "by the numbers" routines—so they do their exercising voluntarily.

They play a lot of handball, which is understandable, since they are a highly competitive group; and a few of them also get in some running and swimming among other seasonal activities.

The Air Force's astronauts, from the beginning of their exercise program, have emphasized endurance training as well as muscle building. Almost without exception they have included running a daily mile or more in addition to their games (usually handball) or loosening-up activities.

However, keeping the astronauts in shape while in space presents an altogether different problem. How do you exercise when you're weightless? The Mercury and Gemini crews tried using a "bungee cord," a rubberized device that they held with their hands and between their feet and stretched, but it was totally inadequate for maintaining condition. The crews all showed some loss of calcium and muscle fitness, as well as cardiovascular deterioration. At least one became light-headed when he was put through some tests after his flight.

Part of the problem, as we have seen, is cramped quarters. But as the spacecraft get larger, and astronauts get some "walking around" room inside the cabin, the longer trips might include some form of ergometer to keep them in condition.

We proved their feasibility in our bed-rest studies. Some of our subjects, who never left the horizontal position, exercised twice daily for 20 days on a special bicycle ergometer strapped to the bed. While the other inactive subjects deteriorated, just as the astronauts do while weightless, the exercisers improved their condition. They actually left their beds in better condition than when they first lay down in them almost three weeks before.

Large spacecraft of the future, when they become permanent space stations or regular commuting vehicles to the moon and beyond, will, I'm convinced, have some such device aboard to keep the astronauts in top condition. Otherwise, their long weightless voyages may exact a penalty and create a problem during extra-vehicular activity and during the critical reentry and recovery phases of the flight.

For the astronauts who plan to fly in these spacecraft, I would recommend a minimum of 50 points per week for optimum preflight conditioning.

OVER 50

BEN KARTMAN was 57 when he was operated on for a bleeding ulcer. The surgeon, who removed four-fifths of his stomach, told him later that he had given him only a 50-50 chance to survive on the operating table.

He did survive and embarked on what I consider a classic case of perseverance.

Ben, now retired, was a magazine editor, and consequently had a desk job most of his life. Worse, he had an almost-traumatic aversion to exercise. An older sister was killed in a playground accident when she was twelve; and his parents, perhaps understandably, would not allow him to participate in any type of athletics.

But it finally caught up with him. He gained weight easily, he was in a stress job, and he was completely inactive. Then came the ulcer and surgery.

When he recovered from the operation and began putting on weight again, he decided to do something about it. And, after nearly sixty years of nothing, it was a monumental task.

Ben went to the huge Lawson YMCA in Chicago and took swimming lessons. And, if Ben demonstrated perseverance, his instructor must have demonstrated the patience of a saint. Let Ben tell it!

"I started in a class twice a week but, at the end of eight weeks, all I could do was shove off and kick my way across the width of the pool at the shallow end. Everyone else in the class was swimming by then."

He quit, but three months later decided to go back and try again, this time with private lessons.

"It was almost a year before I was able to swim in deep water because I had trouble learning the breathing. When I finally got the hang of it, we ended each lesson with my swimming one length—from the deep to the shallow end. After I had done this at least a half-dozen times, one day my instructor said, 'Today, let's do it in the opposite direction.' But I couldn't. The thought that I was heading for deep water caused me to panic."

He tried on five different occasions before he finally made it. One lap, one year after he began.

"My instructor told me afterward that he had me pegged as a hopeless case. He said I had everything against me—my age, my short arms and legs, my lack of coordination, and my fear of the water, which he thought was the worst he had ever seen."

Once Ben had conquered his fear, he began adding laps quite rapidly, and soon started qualifying for the Y's 50-mile club by swimming at least a quarter or half mile on each visit.

"While swimming—and I started going in five days a week—I gradually started losing weight and developing lean muscle. I'm now almost 30 pounds lighter than when I started swimming and I reduced my waistline by 10 inches. My doctor tells me I've added 10 years to my life."

Ben Kartman and I have a mutual friend. The last time they had lunch together, Ben had just celebrated his 66th birthday by qualifying for the Y's 400-mile club. He was in the top ten swimmers at Lawson, and the oldest of the group.

Even though Ben once had a bleeding ulcer, know what he was eating? German sausage and red cabbage and enjoying every mouthful!

So for a man who never exercised before in his life and who nearly died on the operating table, he's doing very well.

Ben Kartman is just one example—just one of many—of a man who turned back the clock when most men his age give up to the "I guess I'm getting old" attitude, and start doing less instead of more, changing their habits to suit their age, instead of keeping or developing active habits and ignoring their age.

As I said, we don't get many of the over-50 types in the Air Force, but the medical literature is bulging with case histories of older men who fought the fight that Ben Kartman fought; and I have had the privilege of working informally with many civilian and retired military people who either began exercise programs late in life, some after serious illnesses, or continued programs begun in their youth.

All of which demonstrates once again, and beyond any question, that the human body is a remarkably resilient instrument. It thrives on use, tends to age prematurely only when we stop using it.

Lt. Col. Robert Morrissey and Lt. Col. (retired) I. J. Newman are the oldest official members of my Poopers' Club, and they represent both groups in the over-50 bracket, the kind who began late and the kind who continued what they'd begun early.

Doctor Morrissey, 52, was putting on weight, falling asleep after dinner and waking up tired in the morning, so he walked over to our clinic and began running.

He's up to two miles now, every day, and showing the results. His weight is down, his alertness up, and his fatigue gone. And the weight loss accomplished one thing most men over 50 can appreciate: "It's easier to button my pants now."

Colonel Newman, 54, now a civil-service psychologist, was typical of the men who had haphazard exercise programs.

"I was in reasonably good shape," he says, "but I was never really sure. I'd exercise or run laps at the YMCA, but I was running without a standard and quit when I felt like it. Now, with the points, I've got some motivation."

The YMCAs have been a blessing to the elderly. Originally aimed at the young, as their name implies, they've attracted a remarkable number of older men in their "Run for your Life" and "Swim for your Life" programs.

One of the most outstanding of these programs began about 10 years ago at the Cleveland (Ohio) YMCA, just about the time the medical fraternity was taking a second look at exercise, not only as preventive medicine, but as curative medicine as well. Cardiac cases, business men in their 50s and 60s, began running in this pioneer Y-sponsored program. And it took courage because some of them were coming off their second and third heart attacks and there was very little encouragement for this sort of thing in medical tradition. The usual advice was to "take it easy," or more colloquially, "act your age." The Cleveland program proved with resounding success that age is no handicap to acting young.

I mention this Cleveland program specifically because it was one of the few where accurate medical data were taken on the participants, before and after their exercise programs. I'll describe some of it when we get to the chapter on clinical conditions. Some of it went beyond pure medicine.

There are other group programs, proving both the interest and the gregarious nature of man. Bill Bowerman, track coach at the University of Oregon and trainer of Olympic distance runners, announced off-handedly that he was forming an informal "joggers" club at the school, but he had to call it off temporarily and reorganize when 1500 people showed up, many of them elderly.

Exercise, however, is basically a lonely avocation, and many of the outstanding oldsters who keep themselves in shape do it alone.

Sports figures, not surprisingly, are well represented. Paavo Nurmi, great Finnish runner of the 1920s, is still running late in life, and Joey Ray, who represented America in three Olympics, is in his mid-60s and still running two miles every day. Famous football coach Amos Alonzo Stagg was running at 96.

Show-business types appreciate the benefits of exercise to keep them active before audiences or cameras. Fred Astaire and Ray Bolger, both in their 60s and both still active, make audiences wonder how they can keep it up. They keep it up by keeping it up, that's how. Rudolph Friml, composer of some all-time great songs such as "Indian Love Call" and "Rose Marie," has outlived some of the stars he wrote them for. Two of them. Nelson Eddy and Jeannette MacDonald are both dead, but Friml, 88, is still alive and still walking, swimming and cycling regularly.

In politics, former President Harry Truman made the morning walk famous, and Michigan Governor George Romney and Wisconsin Senator William Proxmire may make the morning run famous.

One of my favorites, however, is a man I know personally, Paul (Pop) Kepner.

A former Army bandmaster, he retired at 65 and began having heart trouble and back problems and decided to fight back. He started cycling and now, five years later, averages 250 miles a week and has the fitness level of a 40-year-old man! On one occasion, during the New York World's Fair, he cycled from his home in Houston to Washington, D.C. in 11 days, averaging more than 140 miles a day!

On another occasion, Pop competed in a 65-mile marathon race against men whose average age was in the 20s. Pop finished ninth, but was a little disappointed in his performance.

"I rode most of the race with a bad tire," he complained.

I admire these oldsters who can keep going, or get going, when they're past the age of retirement, depending on no one but themselves. But what of those who don't have this spirit?

One such case involved a close friend of mine. His mother had died and he decided that his father, who was not very robust, should move in with him. But, as happens in the military, he received orders for an overseas assignment and didn't think it wise to take his father with him. The only solution seemed to be a nursing home.

"I hated to do it," he told me just before leaving, "but there's no one else to look after him."

He hated it even more when he returned several years later. I ran into him briefly, and inquired about his father.

"He sits," he said bitterly. "He just sits on the porch and stares straight ahead."

This is the real tragedy of growing old, the hopelessness

of being alone and feeling unwanted. It's a typical pattern. Thrown in among strangers, with no one of his own around him, he begins to lose interest in his surroundings, and one of the first things to go is physical activity.

And the symptoms follow.

Already old, he begins to grow older even faster. The unused muscles waste away, losing strength and tone, often just hanging from the bones. The bones themselves become fragile and weak, increasing their susceptibility to fracture. The need to urinate becomes more frequent, increasing the necessity of getting up at odd hours of the night, and further increasing the chances of falling while stumbling around in the dark. The proprioceptive sense, the sense that tells us where our limbs are, fades away so the ability to put his arms and legs where he wants them is diminished, compounding the problem. Sleep itself is fitful.

And as all these symptoms accumulate, it eventually affects his attitude. He just gives up, and loses all resistance to emotional stress. Often such stress produces what is called a "sympathetic storm," an incapacitating reaction that he is unable to cope with. It can be fatal.

I don't blame the nursing homes for what happens to some elderly people, any more than I blame hospitals for what happens to some sick people. Both are receiving stations for someone else's problems.

I do advocate, however, as I have been advocating, that exercise in old age can make the difference between passive despair and active optimism. Physically, it can reverse most of the usual trends of old age, keeping the muscles firm, strengthening the bones, regulating bowel habits, and improving sleep.

Some nursing homes have encouraged exercise. A personal friend operates one such home in Oklahoma. When he went there the patients had the usual attitude, they just wanted to sit around and do nothing. He encouraged those who could to get up and start walking around. He even went to the trouble of changing the landscaping to encourage more activity, planting trees on small hills and asking them to water them so they'd have to climb up and down to get to them.

For those patients who were bedfast, he inquired about our bicycle ergometer, hoping he could strap it to the end of the beds and have them work out on it daily. It's one of the safest ways to get them active; they won't fall down, as they might in walking, or fall off, as they might if it were a real bicycle.

The results from his work thus far have been encouraging. Some bedfast types are up and walking. Others are more active than ever, and all have renewed enthusiasm and self-esteem. They boast to him about their daily accomplishments and, of course, he responds with appropriate remarks.

"Walked around the grounds twice today?" he nods with admiration. "Wonderful, wonderful." And some of these people were brought to him in wheelchairs.

Thirty points might seem like a lot for these oldtimers in their 70s and 80s, but there are so many of them earning their equivalent or more—like Pop Kepner—that I don't see how they can ward off Father Time with less.

WOMEN

"Exercise is one of the basic and effective ways of improving health, achieving physical perfection, preparing for motherhood and the raising of children, and for a highly productive life."

I found this quote in an article on exercise for women, and I agree with every word of it. Unfortunately, the article appeared in a Soviet magazine, and the writer was talking about Russian women.

I wish I could write one for American women and have them believe every word of it.

One of the great disappointments of my career is the general indifference of American women toward exercise. American men are indifferent to it, obviously—four out of five of them are out of shape—but at least they sit home and *worry* about it once in a while. Women don't.

They fall for fads and shortcuts, and spend the time they save on exercise working on their hair or makeup, but they don't really worry about it. A typical reaction is one I got from a young Southern housewife after one of my lectures to an all-female audience. She spent most of the lecture polishing her fingernails, but sought me out afterward.

"Doctor, I don't care about the heart and the lungs and all that. I just want some sweet little exercise that will keep my tummy tucked in."

I tried to explain our running program, and how our men

had lost inches off their waistlines while improving their health, but I didn't get far.

"... and I'm not going to go running around any stupid old track either!"

I'm afraid she missed the point. A lot of women miss the point, and I'd be less than honest if I didn't say it's because the American woman is less interested in her health than in her looks. She won't spend 10 minutes on a track, but she'll spend four hours in a beauty parlor. I just can't get them to understand that if they'd do the things they should to benefit their essential health, they'd benefit their looks as well, especially their figures, and more especially their dispositions. And it's really not that difficult. With the point system, you can be assured of getting maximum benefit with minimum effort.

We have some proof of this.

The Air Force has a WAF (Woman's Air Force) contingent, and some of them participated in our research program. Discounting the difference in sex, and the consequent difference in strength and agility, they showed that women can cope with the point system as easily as men and receive identical training effects. They didn't do nearly as well as the men, of course—only 20 percent made it into the good category for women before training, 45 percent afterward—but most showed improvement, and showed it where it counts.

A heart is a heart, lungs are lungs, and blood vessels are blood vessels. They have no sex and the effect on all are the same. Also, and this pleased the girls most, they changed fat weight to lean weight just as easily as the men do.

The one big difference, as you might guess, was motivation. Most of them just couldn't understand why they should have to run so hard.

"It's not nice to sweat," one said.

"But you sweat when you dance, don't you?"

"Yes, but that's fun!"

Ah, yes. Fun makes sweat acceptable.

Not so many years ago, women accepted sweat as part of their daily life. It was customary for them to do their laundry on a scrub board, and to scour the floor on their hands and knees. Today, push-buttons do most of the chores and women spend more time in front of the television set than their sedentary husbands.

I know of one college coach, who would probably prefer

to remain anonymous, who said, "I get very disgusted when I walk around the campus and see all these fat coeds sitting around. They've already started in on middle age."

If all of this sounds harsh, I have the statistics to prove it. Women used to depend on outliving men as their argument for inactivity, citing housework as the major factor. Today, they still outlive men on the average, but the gap is narrowing. And it's not because men are living longer, it's because women are dying younger. Heart disease is increasing among the weaker sex, and inactivity probably shares the responsibility.

Housework is not the answer, because the sweat-producing housework has been largely replaced by mechanical appliances. And "sweet little exercises" might tuck your tummy in, but they won't build any endurance reserves.

It has to be some form of aerobic exercise, and it has to approach 30 points' worth.

Even if it seems unladylike, and it isn't, I can still recommend running as the best and quickest way to work up a worthwhile sweat and get your points. A nine-minute mile a day would do it, and don't feel too badly about one little old mile. I know of at least one 23-year-old girl who got her start running 15 miles to school every day. She illegally entered the Boston Marathon twice (it's a stag race), running the 26-plus-mile course in less than 3½ hours each time, finishing ahead of a lot of men in the process. Opera-singer Roberta Peters runs regularly in Central Park in New York, claiming it helps her wind.

My wife, Millie, has a regular routine. After she gets me off to work, she puts the baby in a stroller and our dog on a leash and, pushing one and dragging the other, she runs through the streets of our suburban neighborhood. And she's doing very well. She came out to our lab once to do the 12-minute test, and without baby or dog she ran 1.30 miles.

If running is not your cup of tea, however, swimming is second best and definitely ladylike. You can wear your pretty bathing suit and socialize around the pool. And you can do it the rest of your life. Actress Gladys Cooper for one, who readily admits to being in her mid-70s (and doesn't look it)—you may remember her as Mrs. Higgins in the movie version of "My Fair Lady"—swims every day, rain or shine, and has been doing so since childhood.

Cycling is certainly ladylike, and definitely beneficial

healthwise. It offers another chance for sports clothes, and is great for socializing, taking trips with your friends or your husband.

Rope skipping, which used to be a girls' sport in my childhood, is also a good route to fitness (see Appendix, page 173), and can be done at home. So can running-in-place.

There are many others, easily adaptable to women, such as golf, tennis, skating and skiing where you can easily pick up enough points to fill out a week—and have fun doing it. And there is always walking.

So there is hardly any excuse for hiding behind your sex as a means of avoiding exercise. It's your health, and health has no sex.

Besides the physical benefits, you might notice some change in personality.

Some members of the Poopers' Club do their running near their homes, and the wives drive them either to the park or track, and follow them around in the car as they run. A few got tired of that, and climbed out and started running, too. They noticed the usual changes, losing weight, improving sleep, toughening up.

One of them said, "I'm so relaxed now, I'm not as mean as I used to be."

I'll settle for that.

7: The Training Effect

A FRIEND of mine in private practice was physician to a prominent man in the Midwest who died after a long illness. He was trying to describe what happened to a local reporter.

"A plaque broke loose from the lining of an artery, obstructing a coronary vessel and producing a myocardial infarction," he said. "His ECG revealed acute ischemic changes, manifested by changes in the S-T segment and T waves. The cause of death was ventricular fibrillation, terminating in a cardiac arrest."

The young reporter stared at him, bug-eyed. Finally, he rubbed his hand over his head and said, "Doc, I'm just a poor country boy trying to get along in the world. Would you mind translating some of that into newspaper language?

"Certainly. The man had a heart attack."

"Oh."

This breakdown in communication between doctors and laymen is not uncommon. It happens to me all the time. We're involved in this medical data daily and sometimes it's hard to shift gears. As one medical writer told me, "I've never met a doctor yet who talked English."

I mention this here because I'm about to begin what I promised earlier, to give you the medical detail of what happens to the human body in response to aerobic exercises.

In this chapter, on the training effect, I will detail the phys-

THE AEROBICS POINT SYSTEM

● If you are 35 years of age or under, take the initial 12-minute test for the determination of your fitness category unless you have some known medical problem.

● If you are over 35 years of age and *have been* exercising regularly (that is, at least three times a week for a minimum of six weeks), take the initial 12-minute test.

● If you are over 35 years of age and *have not been* exercising regularly. do not take the initial 12-minute test. Place yourself in one of the Category I programs (pages 2-7) and begin exercising without testing

---

What is the distance you can cover in 12 minutes?

What is your fitness category?

IF YOU COVER:	YOU ARE IN FITNESS CATEGORY:
less than 1.0 mile	I Very Poor
1.0 to 1.24 miles	II Poor
1.25 to 1.49 miles	III Fair
1.50 to 1.74 miles	IV Good
1.75 miles or more	V Excellent

Now turn to

the Exercise Program *of your choice*

under your Fitness Category:

	I	II	III	IV/V
Running	page 2	8	14	20
Swimming	3	9	15	20
Cycling	4	10	16	20
Walking	5	11	17	20
Stationary Running	6	12	18	20
Handball/Squash/Basketball	7	13	19	20

Exercise Programs—Category I

RUNNING

WEEK	DISTANCE (miles)	WALK/RUN	TIME GOAL (minutes)	FREQ/WK	POINTS/WK
1	1.0	Walk	13:30	5	10
2	1.0	Walk	13:00	5	10
3	1.0	Walk	12:45	5	10
4	1.0	W/R	11:45	5	15
5	1.0	W/R	11:00	5	15
6	1.0	W/R	10:30	5	15
7	1.0	Run	9:45	5	20
8	1.0	Run	9:30	5	20
9	1.0	Run	9:15	5	20
10	1.0 and 1.5	Run Run	9:00 16:00	3 2	21
11	1.0 and 1.5	Run Run	8:45 15:00	3 2	21
12	1.0 and 1.5	Run Run	8:30 14:00	3 2	24
13	1.0 and 1.5	Run Run	8:15 13:30	3 2	24
14	1.0 and 1.5	Run Run	7:55 13:00	3 2	27
15	1.0 and 1.5 and 2.0	Run Run Run	7:45 12:30 18:00	2 2 1	30
16	1.5 and 2.0	Run Run	11:55 17:00	2 2	31

After completing the 16 week program, go to page 20 and select one of the 30 point per week programs or develop one of your own from the point value charts beginning on page 23.

Exercise Programs—Category I

SWIMMING

WEEK	DISTANCE (yards)	SWIM	TIME GOAL (minutes)	FREQ/WK	POINTS/WK
1	100	Swim	2:30	5	6
2	150	Swim	3:00	5	7½
3	200	Swim	4:00	5	7½
4	250	Swim	5:30	5	10
5	250	Swim	5:00	5	10
6	300	Swim	6:00	5	12½
7	300	Swim	6:00	5	12½
8	400	Swim	8:30	5	17½
9	400	Swim	8:30	5	17½
10	400 and 500	Swim Swim	8:00 10:30	2 3	19
11	400 and 600	Swim Swim	8:00 12:30	2 3	22
12	500 and 700	Swim Swim	10:30 15:30	3 2	24
13	600 and 800	Swim Swim	12:30 16:30	3 2	25
14	600 and 800	Swim Swim	12:30 16:00	2 3	29½
15	700	Swim	15:00	5	30
16	1000	Swim	20:30	4	34

After completing the 16 week program, go to page 20 and select one of the 30 point per week programs or develop one of your own from the point value charts beginning on page 23.

Exercise Programs—Category I

CYCLING

WEEK	DISTANCE (miles)	CYCLE	TIME GOAL (minutes)	FREQ/WK	POINTS/WK
1	2.0	Cycle	10:00	5	5
2	2.0	Cycle	9:00	5	5
3	2.0	Cycle	7:45	5	10
4	3.0	Cycle	11:50	5	15
5	3.0	Cycle	11:00	5	15
6	3.0	Cycle	10:30	5	15
7	4.0	Cycle	15:45	5	20
8	4.0	Cycle	15:30	5	20
9	4.0	Cycle	14:30	5	20
10	4.0 and 5.0	Cycle Cycle	14:00 18:30	4 1	21
11	4.0 and 5.0	Cycle Cycle	14:00 18:00	3 2	22
12	4.0 and 6.0	Cycle Cycle	13:45 23:30	3 2	24
13	4.0 and 6.0	Cycle Cycle	13:30 23:00	3 2	24
14	5.0 and 6.0	Cycle Cycle	17:00 22:00	3 2	27
15	6.0	Cycle	21:00	5	30
16	8.0	Cycle	28:30	4	32

After completing the 16 week program, go to page 20 and select one of the 30 point per week programs or develop one of your own from the point value charts beginning on page 23.

WALKING

WEEK	DISTANCE (miles)	WALK	TIME GOAL (minutes)	FREQ/WK	POINTS/WK
1	1.0	Walk	15:00	5	5
2	1.0	Walk	14:00	5	10
3	1.0	Walk	13:45	5	10
4	1.5	Walk	21:30	5	15
5	1.5	Walk	21:00	5	15
6	1.5	Walk	20:30	5	15
7	2.0	Walk	28:00	5	20
8	2.0	Walk	27:45	5	20
9	2.0	Walk	27:30	5	20
10	2.0 and 2.5	Walk Walk	27:30 35:30	3 2	22
11	2.0 and 2.5	Walk Walk	27:30 35:00	3 2	22
12	2.5 and 3.0	Walk Walk	34:30 41:30	4 1	26
13	2.5 and 3.0	Walk Walk	33:15 42:00	3 2	27
14	2.5 and 3.0	Walk Walk	33:00 41:30	3 2	27
15	3.0	Walk	42:00	5	30
16	4.0	Walk	56:00	4	32

After completing the 16 week program, go to page 20 and select one of the 30 point per week programs or develop one of your own from the point value charts beginning on page 23.

STATIONARY RUNNING

WEEK	DURATION (minutes)	FREQ (steps/min.)	FREQ/WK	POINTS/WK
1	2:30	70—80	5	4
2	2:30	70—80	5	4
3	5:00	70—80	5	10
4	5:00	70—80	5	10
5	7:30	70—80	5	11¼
6	7:30	70—80	5	11¼
7	10:00	70—80	5	15
8	10:00	70—80	5	15
9	12:30	70—80	5	18¾
10	12:30	70—80	5	18¾
11	15:00	70—80	5	22½
12	10:00 (1 x in a.m.) and 10:00 (1 x in p.m.)	70—80 70—80	2	25½
	and 15:00	70—80	3	
13	12:30 (1 x in a.m.) and 12:30 (1 x in p.m.)	70—80 70—80	2	28½
	and 15:00	70—80	3	
14	12:30 (1 x in a.m.) and 12:30 (1 x in p.m.)	70—80 70—80	2	28½
	and 15:00	70—80	3	
15	20:00	70—80	5	30
16	20:00	80—90	4	32

After completing the 16 week program, go to page 20 and select one of the 30 point per week programs or develop one of your own from the point value charts beginning on page 23.

Exercise Programs—Category I

HANDBALL/SQUASH/BASKETBALL*

WEEK	TIME (min.)	FREQ/WK	POINTS/WK
1	10	5	7½
2	15	5	11¼
3	15	5	11¼
4	20	5	15
5	20	5	15
6	20	5	15
7	30	5	22½
8	30	5	22½
9	30	5	22½
10	35	5	26¼
11	35	5	26¼
12	35 and 40	3 2	27¼
13	35 and 40	3 2	27¼
14	30 and 45	2 3	29¼
15	40	5	30
16	50	4	30

*Continuous exercise. Do not count breaks, etc.

After completing the 16 week program, go to page 20 and select one of the 30 point per week programs or develop one of your own from the point value charts beginning on page 23.

Exercise Programs—Category II

RUNNING

WEEK	DISTANCE (miles)	WALK/RUN	TIME GOAL (minutes)	FREQ/WK	POINTS/WK
1	1.0	Walk	13:30	5	10
2	1.0	Walk	12:45	5	10
3	1.0	W/R	11:45	5	15
4	1.0	W/R	11:00	5	15
5	1.0	W/R	10:30	5	15
6	1.0	Run	9:45	5	20
7	1.0	Run	9:15	5	20
8	1.0 and	Run	9:00	3	21
	1.5	Run	16:00	2	
9	1.0 and	Run	8:45	3	21
	1.5	Run	15:00	2	
10	1.0 and	Run	8:15	3	24
	1.5	Run	13:30	2	
11	1.0 and	Run	7:55	3	27
	1.5	Run	13:00	2	
12	1.0 and	Run	7:45	2	30
	1.5 and	Run	12:30	2	
	2.0	Run	18:00	1	
13	1.5 and	Run	11:55	2	31
	2.0	Run	17:00	2	

After completing the 13 week program, go to page 20 and select one of the 30 point per week programs or develop one of your own from the point value charts beginning on page 23.

Exercise Programs—Category II

SWIMMING

WEEK	DISTANCE (yards)	SWIM	TIME GOAL (minutes)	FREQ/WK	POINTS/WK
1	100	Swim	2:30	5	6
2	200	Swim	4:00	5	7½
3	250	Swim	5:30	5	10
4	250	Swim	5:00	5	10
5	300	Swim	6:00	5	12½
6	300	Swim	6:00	5	12½
7	400	Swim	8:30	5	17½
8	400 and	Swim	8:00	2	19
	500	Swim	10:30	3	
9	400 and	Swim	8:00	2	22
	600	Swim	12:30	3	
10	600 and	Swim	12:30	3	25
	800	Swim	16:30	2	
11	600 and	Swim	12:30	2	29½
	800	Swim	16:00	3	
12	700	Swim	15:00	5	30
13	1000	Swim	20:30	4	34

After completing the 13 week program, go to page 20 and select one of the 30 point per week programs or develop one of your own from the point value charts beginning on page 23.

CYCLING

WEEK	DISTANCE (miles)	CYCLE	TIME GOAL (minutes)	FREQ/WK	POINTS/WK
1	2.0	Cycle	10:00	5	5
2	2.0	Cycle	7:45	5	10
3	3.0	Cycle	11:50	5	15
4	3.0	Cycle	11:00	5	15
5	3.0	Cycle	10:30	5	15
6	4.0	Cycle	15:45	5	20
7	4.0	Cycle	14:30	5	20
8	4.0 and 5.0	Cycle Cycle	14:00 18:30	4 1	21
9	4.0 and 5.0	Cycle Cycle	14:00 18:00	3 2	22
10	4.0 and 6.0	Cycle Cycle	13:30 23:00	3 2	24
11	5.0 and 6.0	Cycle Cycle	17:00 22:00	3 2	27
12	6.0	Cycle	21:00	5	30
13	8.0	Cycle	28:30	4	32

After completing the 13 week program, go to page 20 and select one of the 30 point per week programs or develop one of your own from the point value charts beginning on page 23.

Exercise Programs—Category II

WALKING

WEEK	DISTANCE (miles)	WALK	TIME GOAL (minutes)	FREQ/WK	POINTS/WK
1	1.0	Walk	15:00	5	5
2	1.0	Walk	13:45	5	10
3	1.5	Walk	21:30	5	15
4	1.5	Walk	21:00	5	15
5	1.5	Walk	20:30	5	15
6	2.0	Walk	28:00	5	20
7	2.0	Walk	27:30	5	20
8	2.0 and 2.5	Walk Walk	27:30 35:30	3 2	22
9	2.0 and 2.5	Walk Walk	27:30 35:00	3 2	22
10	2.5 and 3.0	Walk Walk	33:15 42:00	3 2	27
11	2.5 and 3.0	Walk Walk	33:00 41:30	3 2	27
12	3.0	Walk	42:00	5	30
13	4.0	Walk	56:00	4	32

After completing the 13 week program, go to page 20 and select one of the 30 point per week programs or develop one of your own from the point value charts beginning on page 23.

STATIONARY RUNNING

WEEK	DURATION (minutes)	FREQ (steps/min.)	FREQ/WK	POINTS/WK
1	[2:30]	70—80	5	4
2	5:00	70—80	5	10
3	5:00	70—80	5	10
4	7:30	70—80	5	11¼
5	7:30	70—80	5	11¼
6	10:00	70—80	5	15
7	12:30	70—80	5	18¾
8	12:30	70—80	5	18¾
9	15:00	70—80	5	22½
10	12:30 (1 x in a.m.) and 12:30 (1 x in p.m.)	70—80 70—80	2	
	and 15:00	70—80	3	28½
11	12:30 (1 x in a.m.) and 12:30 (1 x in p.m.)	70—80 70—80	2	
	and 15:00	70—80	3	28½
12	20:00	70—80	5	30
13	20:00	80—90	4	32

After completing the 13 week program, go to page 20 and select one of the 30 point per week programs or develop one of your own from the point value charts beginning on page 23.

Exercise Programs—Category II

HANDBALL/SQUASH/BASKETBALL*

WEEK	TIME (min.)	FREQ/WK	POINTS/WK
1	10	5	7½
2	15	5	11¼
3	20	5	15
4	20	5	15
5	20	5	15
6	30	5	22½
7	30	5	22½
8	35	5	26¼
9	35	5	26¼
10	35 and 40	3 2	27¼
11	30 and 45	2 3	29¼
12	40	5	30
13	50	4	30

*Continuous exercise. Do not count breaks, etc.

After completing the 13 week program, go to page 20 and select one of the 30 point per week programs or develop one of your own from the point value charts beginning on page 23.

Exercise Programs—Category III

RUNNING

WEEK	DISTANCE (miles)	WALK/RUN	TIME GOAL (minutes)	FREQ/WK	POINTS/WK
1	1.0	Walk	12:45	5	10
2	1.0	W/R	11:00	5	15
3	1.0	W/R	10:30	5	15
4	1.0	Run	9:30	5	20
5	1.0	Run	9:15	5	20
6	1.0 and	Run	8:45	3	21
	1.5	Run	15:00	2	
7	1.0 and	Run	8:30	3	24
	1.5	Run	14:00	2	
8	1.0 and	Run	7:55	3	27
	1.5	Run	13:00	2	
9	1.0 and	Run	7:45	2	
	1.5 and	Run	12:30	2	30
	2.0	Run	18:00	1	
10	1.5 and	Run	11:55	2	31
	2.0	Run	17:00	2	

After completing the 10 week program, go to page 20 and select one of the 30 point per week programs or develop one of your own from the point value charts beginning on page 23.

SWIMMING

WEEK	DISTANCE (yards)	SWIM	TIME GOAL (minutes)	FREQ/WK	POINTS/WK
1	200	Swim	4:00	5	7½
2	250	Swim	5:00	5	10
3	300	Swim	6:00	5	12½
4	400	Swim	8:30	5	17½
5	400	Swim	8:30	5	17½
6	400 and 600	Swim Swim	8:00 12:30	2 3	22
7	500 and 700	Swim Swim	10:30 15:30	3 2	24
8	600 and 800	Swim Swim	12:30 16:00	2 3	29½
9	700	Swim	15:00	5	30
10	1000	Swim	20:30	4	34

After completing the 10 week program, go to page 20 and select one of the 30 point per week programs or develop one of your own from the point value charts beginning on page 23.

CYCLING

WEEK	DISTANCE (miles)	CYCLE	TIME GOAL (minutes)	FREQ/WK	POINTS/WK
1	2.0	Cycle	7:45	5	10
2	3.0	Cycle	11:00	5	15
3	3.0	Cycle	10:30	5	15
4	4.0	Cycle	15:30	5	20
5	4.0	Cycle	14:30	5	20
6	4.0 and	Cycle	14:00	3	22
	5.0	Cycle	18:00	2	
7	4.0 and	Cycle	13:45	3	24
	6.0	Cycle	23:30	2	
8	5.0 and	Cycle	17:00	3	27
	6.0	Cycle	22:00	2	
9	6.0	Cycle	21:00	5	30
10	8.0	Cycle	28:30	4	32

After completing the 10 week program, go to page 20 and select one of the 30 point per week programs or develop one of your own from the point value charts beginning on page 23.

Exercise Programs—Category III

WALKING

WEEK	DISTANCE (miles)	WALK	TIME GOAL (mnutes)	FREQ/WK	POINTS/WK
1	1.0	Walk	13:45	5	10
2	1.5	Walk	21:00	5	15
3	1.5	Walk	20:30	5	15
4	2.0	Walk	27:45	5	20
5	2.0	Walk	27:30	5	20
6	2.0 and 2.5	Walk Walk	27:30 35:00	3 2	22
7	2.5 and 3.0	Walk Walk	34:30 41:30	4 1	26
8	2.5 and 3.0	Walk Walk	33:00 41:30	3 2	27
9	3.0	Walk	42:00	5	30
10	4.0	Walk	56:00	4	32

After completing the 10 week program, go to page 20 and select one of the 30 points per week programs or develop one of your own from the point value charts beginning on page 23.

STATIONARY RUNNING

WEEK	DURATION (minutes)	FREQ (steps/min.)	FREQ/WK	POINTS/WK
1	5:00	70—80	5	10
2	7:30	70—80	5	11¼
3	7:30	70—80	5	11¼
4	10:00	70—80	5	15
5	12:30	70—80	5	18¾
6	15:00	70—80	5	22½
7	10:00 (1 x in a.m.) and 10:00 (1 x in p.m.) and	70—80 70—80	2	25½
	15:00	70—80	3	
8	12:30 (1 x in a.m.) and 12:30 (1 x in p.m.) and	70—80 70—80	2	28½
	15:00	70—80	3	
9	20:00	70—80	5	30
10	20:00	80—90	4	32

After completing the 10 week program, go to page 20 and select one of the 30 point per week programs or develop one of your own from the point value charts beginning on page 23.

Exercise Programs—Category III

HANDBALL/SQUASH/BASKETBALL*

WEEK	TIME (min.)	FREQ/WK	POINTS/WK
1	15	5	11¼
2	20	5	15
3	20	5	15
4	30	5	22½
5	30	5	22½
6	35	5	26¼
7	35 and 40	3 2	27¼
8	30 and 45	2 3	29¼
9	40	5	30
10	50	4	30

*Continuous exercise. Do not count breaks, etc.

After completing the 10 week program, go to page 20 and select one of the 30 point per week programs or develop one of your own from the point value charts beginning on page 23.

Exercise Programs—Categories IV and V

Fitness level is satisfactory—only requirement is to maintain fitness using one of the following programs:

Running	DISTANCE (miles)	TIME GOAL (minutes)	FREQ/WK	POINTS/WK
	1.0	under 8:00	6	30
	or			
	1.0	under 6:30	5	30
	or			
	1.5	under 12:00	4	30
	or			
	2.0	under 16:00	3	30

Swimming	(yards)			
	500	8:20-12:29	8	32
	or			
	600	10:00-14:59	6	30
	or			
	800	13:20-19:59	5	32
	or			
	1000	16:40-24:59	4	34

Cycling	(miles)			
	5.0	15:00-19:59	6	30
	or			
	6.0	18:00-23:59	5	30
	or			
	8.0	24:00-31:59	4	32
	or			
	10.0	30:00-39:59	3	30

Walking	(miles)			
	2.0	24:00-29:00	8	32
	or			
	3.0	36:00-43:30	5	30
	or			
	4.0	48:00-58:00	4	32
	or			
	5.0	60:00-72:30	3	30

Stationary Running	DURATION (min.)	FREQ (steps/min.)		
	10:00 in a.m. &	70—80 ⎫	5	30
	10:00 in p.m.	70—80 ⎭		
	or			
	15:00	70—80	7	30
	or			
	15:00	80—90	5	30
	or			
	20:00	80—90	4	32

Handball Squash Basketball	TIME (min.)*		
	40	5	30
	or		
	50	4	30
	or		
	70	3	30

*Continuous exercise. Do not count breaks, etc.

Suggested Walking Program for Cardiac Patients—A
(minimal disease—uncomplicated)

WEEKS	DISTANCE (miles)	WALK	TIME GOAL (minutes)	FREQ/WK	POINTS/WK
1-2	1.0	Walk	15:00	5	5
3-4	1.0	Walk	14:00	5	10
5-6	1.0	Walk	13:45	5	10
7-8	1.5	Walk	21.30	5	15
9-10	1.5	Walk	21:00	5	15
11-12	1.5	Walk	20:30	5	15
13-14	2.0	Walk	28:00	5	20
15-16	2.0	Walk	27:45	5	20
17-18	2.0	Walk	27:30	5	20
19-20	2.0 2.5	Walk Walk	27:30 33:45	3} 2}	22
21-22	2.0 2.5	Walk Walk	27:30 33:30	3} 2}	22
23-24	2.5 3.0	Walk Walk	33:15 41:30	4} 1}	26
25-26	2.5 3.0	Walk Walk	33:15 41:15	3} 2}	27
27-28	2.5 3.0	Walk Walk	33:00 40:00	3} 2}	27
29-30	3.0	Walk	41:00	5	30
31-32	4.0	Walk	55:00	4	32

Minimum Requirements to Maintain Fitness
After Completion of Conditioning Program

	DISTANCE	WALK	TIME GOAL	FREQ/WK	POINTS/WK
	2.0	Walk	24:00-28:59	8	32
or	3.0	Walk	36:00-43:29	5	30
or	4.0	Walk	48:00-57:59	4	32
or	5.0	Walk	60:00-72:29	3	30

Suggested Walking Program for Cardiac Patients—B
(moderate disease)

WEEKS	DISTANCE (miles)	WALK	TIME GOAL (minutes)	FREQ/WK	POINTS/WK
1-2	1.0	Walk	20:00	5	0
3-4	1.0	Walk	18:00	5	5
5-6	1.0	Walk	15:00	5	5
7-8	1.5	Walk	24:00	5	7½
9-10	1.5	Walk	23:00	5	7½
11-12	1.5	Walk	21:45	5	7½
13-14	2.0	Walk	29:30	5	10
15-16	2.0	Walk	29:00	5	10
17-18	1.5 2.0	Walk Walk	21:45 28:00	2} 3}	15
19-20	1.5 2.0	Walk Walk	21:00 28:00	2} 3}	18
21-22	2.0 2.5	Walk Walk	28:00 35:00	3} 2}	22
23-24	2.5 3.0	Walk Walk	35:00 43:00	4} 1}	26
25-26	2.5 3.0	Walk Walk	34:30 42:00	3} 2}	27
27-28	2.5 3.0	Walk Walk	34:00 41:30	3} 2}	27
29-30	3.0	Walk	41:00	5	30
31-32	4.0	Walk	55:00	4	32

Minimum Requirements to Maintain Fitness
After Completion of Conditioning Program

	DISTANCE	WALK	TIME GOAL	FREQ/WK	POINTS/WK
	2.0	Walk	24:00-28:59	8	32
	or 3.0	Walk	36:00-43:29	5	30
	or 4.0	Walk	48:00-57:59	4	32
	or 5.0	Walk	60:00-72:29	3	30

Point Value Charts

RUNNING

For a more complete breakdown of these point values, see Appendix.

1.0 Mile	POINTS
19:59—14:30 min.	1
14:29—12:00 min.	2
11:59—10:00 min.	3
9:59— 8:00 min.	4
7:59— 6:30 min.	5
under 6:30 min.	6

1.5 Miles	
29:59—21:45 min.	1½
21:44—18:00 min.	3
17:59—15:00 min.	4½
14:59—12:00 min.	6
11:59— 9:45 min.	7½
under 9:45 min.	9

2.0 Miles	
40:00 min. or longer	1*
39:59—29:00 min.	2
28:59—24:00 min.	4
23:59—20:00 min.	6
19:59—16:00 min.	8
15:59—13:00 min.	10
under 13:00 min.	12

2.5 Miles	
50:00 min. or longer	1*
49:59—36:15 min.	2½
36:14—30:00 min.	5
29:59—25:00 min.	7½
24:59—20:00 min.	10
19:59—16:15 min.	12½
under 16:15 min.	15

3.0 Miles	POINTS
60:00 min. or longer	1½*
59:59—43:30 min.	3
43:29—36:00 min.	6
35:59—30:00 min.	9
29:59—24:00 min.	12
23:59—19:30 min.	15
under 19:30 min.	18

4.0 Miles	
80:00 min. or longer	2*
79:59—58:00 min.	4
57:59—48:00 min.	8
47:59—40:00 min.	12
39:59—32:00 min.	16
31:59—26:00 min.	20
under 26:00 min.	24

5.0 Miles	
100:00 min. or longer	2½*
99:59—72:30 min.	5
72:29—60:00 min.	10
59:59—50:00 min.	15
49:59—40:00 min.	20
39:59—32:30 min.	25
under 32:30 min.	30

*Exercise of sufficient duration to be of cardiovascular benefit. At this speed, ordinarily no training effect would occur. However, the duration is of such extent that a training effect does begin to occur.

SWIMMING

For a more complete breakdown of these point values, see Appendix.

200 Yards	POINTS	600 Yards	POINTS
6:40 min. or longer	0	20:00 min. or longer	1½*
6:39— 5:00 min.	1	19:59—15:00 min.	4
4:59— 3:20 min.	1½	14:59—10:00 min.	5
under 3:20 min.	2½	under 10:00 min.	7½

300 Yards		700 Yards	
10:00 min. or longer	1*	23:20 min. or longer	1½*
9:59— 7:30 min.	1½	23:19—17:30 min.	4½
7:29— 5:00 min.	2½	17:29—11:40 min.	6
under 5:00 min.	3½	under 11:40 min.	8½

400 Yards		800 Yards	
13:20 min. or longer	1*	26:40 min. or longer	1½*
13:19—10:00 min.	2½	26:39—20:00 min.	5
9:59— 6:40 min.	3½	19:59—13:20 min.	6½
under 6:40 min.	5	under 13:20 min.	10

500 Yards		1000 Yards	
16:40 min. or longer	1*	33:20 min. or longer	2*
16:39—12:30 min.	3	33:19—25:00 min.	6¼
12:29— 8:20 min.	4	24:59—16:40 min.	8½
under 8:20 min.	6	under 16:40 min.	12½

*Exercise of sufficient duration to be of cardiovascular benefit. At this speed, ordinarily no training effect would occur. However, the duration is of such extent that a training effect does begin to occur.

Point Value Charts

CYCLING

For a more complete breakdown of these point values, see Appendix.

2 Miles	POINTS	6 Miles	POINTS
12 min. or longer	0	36 min. or longer	1*
11:59— 8:00 min.	1	35:59—24:00 min.	3
7:59— 6:00 min.	2	23:59—18:00 min.	6
under 6:00 min.	3	under 18:00 min.	9

3 Miles		8 Miles	
18 min. or longer	0	48 min. or longer	1½*
17:59—12:00 min.	1½	47:59—32:00 min.	4
11:59— 9:00 min.	3	31:59—24:00 min.	8
under 9:00 min.	4½	under 24:00 min.	12

4 Miles		10 Miles	
24 min. or longer	0	60 min. or longer	2*
23:59—16:00 min.	2	59:59—40:00 min.	5
15:59—12:00 min.	4	39:59—30:00 min.	10
under 12:00 min.	6	under 30:00 min.	15

5 Miles	
30 min. or longer	1*
29:59—20:00 min.	2½
19:59—15:00 min.	5
under 15:00 min.	7½

*Exercise of sufficient duration to be of cardiovascular benefit. At this speed, ordinarily no training effect would occur. However, the duration is of such extent that a training effect does begin to occur.

Point Value Charts

WALKING

For a more complete breakdown of these point values, see Appendix.

1.0 Mile	POINTS		3.0 Miles	POINTS
19:59—14:30 min.	1		60:00 min. or longer	1½*
14:29—12:00 min.	2		59:59—43:30 min.	3
			43:29—36:00 min.	6
1.5 Miles				
29:59—21:45 min.	1½		**4.0 Miles**	
21:44—18:00 min.	3		80:00 min. or longer	2*
			79:59—58:00 min.	4
2.0 Miles			57:59—48:00 min.	8
40:00 min. or longer	1*			
39:59—29:00 min.	2		**5.0 Miles**	
28:59—24:00 min.	4		100:00 min. or longer	2½*
			99:59—72:30 min.	5
2.5 Miles			72:29—60:00 min.	10
50:00 min. or longer	1*			
49:59—36:15 min.	2½			
36:14—30:00 min.	5			

*Exercise of sufficient duration to be of cardiovascular benefit. At this speed, ordinarily no training effect would occur. However, the duration is of such extent that a training effect does begin to occur.

Point Value Charts

STATIONARY RUNNING

For a more complete breakdown of these point values, see Appendix.

TIME	*60-70 STEPS/MIN	POINTS	*70-80 STEPS/MIN	POINTS	*80-90 STEPS/MIN	POINTS
2:30			175-200	¾	200-225	1
5:00	300-350	1¼	350-400	1½	400-450	2
7:30			525-600	2¼	600-675	3
10:00	600-700	2½	700-800	3	800-900	4
12:30			875-1000	3¾	1000-1125	5
15:00	900-1050	3¾	1000-1200	4½	1200-1350	6
17:30			1225-1400	5¼	1400-1575	7
20:00	1200-1400	5	1400-1600	6	1600-1800	8

*Count only when the left foot hits the floor. Knees must be brought up in front raising the feet at least 8 inches from the floor.

Point Value Charts

HANDBALL/SQUASH/BASKETBALL*

For a more complete breakdown of these point values, see Appendix.

DURATION	POINTS	DURATION	POINTS
10 min.	1½	55 min.	8¼
15 min.	2¼	60 min.	9
20 min.	3	65 min.	9¾
25 min.	3¾	70 min.	10½
30 min.	4½	75 min.	11¼
35 min.	5¼	80 min.	12
40 min.	6	85 min.	12¾
45 min.	6¾	90 min.	13½
50 min.	7½		

*Continuous exercise. Do not include breaks, etc.

PERSONAL PROGRESS CHART

DATE	EXERCISE	DISTANCE	DURATION	POINTS	CUMULAT. POINTS

PERSONAL PROGRESS CHART

DATE	EXERCISE	DISTANCE	DURATION	POINTS	CUMULAT. POINTS

PERSONAL PROGRESS CHART

DATE	EXERCISE	DISTANCE	DURATION	POINTS	CUMULAT. POINTS

PERSONAL PROGRESS CHART

DATE	EXERCISE	DISTANCE	DURATION	POINTS	CUMULAT. POINTS

iological responses to training, or the reaction of the bodily systems to the proper amount of aerobics.

In the next chapter, on clinical conditions (like heart attacks), I shall detail how, and why, the bodily systems succumb to illness and disease, and how they can, and sometimes do, come back in response to an intelligent program of aerobics.

And I'll try to translate all of it into English.

To begin, it's necessary to recall that oxygen is the key to understanding what happens. Getting oxygen to the body tissue is the rock-bottom basis of conditioning, and it's convenient to think of the systems that process and deliver oxygen as one huge, magnificent, wondrous assembly line, complete with receiving lines to dispose of wastes, and the most beautiful engine ever conceived to keep all of it moving.

If you're ready, let's take a trip through your body and see how the whole process works.

THE LUNGS

It all begins here. This is where the air you breathe is processed and the oxygen removed and transferred to the blood stream for distribution throughout your body. And the amount of air that your lungs can process is the first limiting factor on your condition.

To understand how conditioned lungs can process more air, it's necessary to understand the process. The lungs are like a dairy where bulk milk comes in, cream is separated from it, then bottled and set off on an assembly line for distribution. Empties come back on another assembly line, are flushed out then returned to the first assembly line to receive more cream and start the process all over again.

Oxygen is the cream of the air we breathe. When bulk air comes into your lungs, the oxygen is extracted from it, "bottled" in red-blood cells—specifically, in the hemoglobin inside the cells—then sent off on the assembly line of the blood stream for distribution. When they reach the tissue, the "bottles" exchange oxygen for carbon dioxide, then carry the wastes back to the lungs where they are flushed out. The "bottles" are then ready to pick up more oxygen and start the process all over again.

The air we breathe is approximately 21 percent oxygen and

79 percent nitrogen, with negligible traces of other gases, and the ratio never varies. What does vary is the amount of air we can process. If your lungs can't process enough air, they can't extract enough oxygen to produce enough energy, and there are two factors limiting the lungs' ability to process air.

First, the lungs have no muscles of their own, but are completely dependent for expansion and contraction on the muscles of the rib cage and the diaphragm. As you sit there, breathing in and out, this is what is going on. As you inhale, the muscles surrounding the lungs create a larger area in the lung cavity—a partial vacuum, actually—so the air, aided by atmospheric pressure, just rushes in. When exhaling, the muscles, aided somewhat by the natural elasticity of your lungs and chest wall, actually force the air out against atmospheric pressure. So, inhaling, the air is being pushed in; exhaling, it is being pushed out.

This is all with the body at rest, and you'll recall all bodies at rest consume basically the same amount of oxygen, and consequently inhale and exhale just about the same amounts of air. Now, as you move into action, the amount of air you can inhale and exhale is limited, first by the size of the vacuum your muscles can create for the lungs to expand into, and secondly by the size of the area they can be squeezed back into.

Obviously, a conditioned man, as he moves into action, has the capability for inhaling more air, and for longer periods, and of exhaling more wastes, because the muscles around his lungs have been trained to do more work.

One of the most outstanding, and inspiring, examples of the work the muscles around the lungs can do was exemplified in a young airman I came across at Lackland. He was in a group participating in one of our frequent field tests there and, when I saw him, my jaw dropped. He had a congenital defect. Most of the muscles on the right side of his chest cavity were missing. He was born without them, and in that area, he was literally "just skin and bones."

Out of earshot, I asked one of the instructors, "How did he ever get into service?"

The instructor shrugged. "He's a volunteer, and I guess he passed the minimum requirements and got a waiver on the rest."

I walked over to the boy and asked him if he was sure he wanted to go through with the test.

He just smiled and said, "Yes, sir."

I ran with the group that day, and kept my eye on him. It was agonizing, but awesome, to watch. He ran with his upper body leaning almost at a 45-degree angle to the right, his left shoulder heaving up and down as whatever rib muscles he had, worked overtime to force air in and out of his lungs. Every once in a while, I'd call out over my shoulder, "You all right?"

"Just fine, sir, just fine."

He did just fine, too. After conditioning, and with only 55 percent of his predicted usable lung space, he worked up to 50 points a week, raised his oxygen consumption to 49 ml's min, and his 12-minute test to 1.68—running it in combat boots!

I remember this case each time I see one of our sterling citizens, born with a healthy body, running for a bus and running out of breath within a block. In disgust, all I can mutter to myself is, "If you're not going to take care of what you have, why don't you give it to someone who would?"

All this is related to the condition of the muscles surrounding the lungs. The second limiting factor on how much air your lungs can process is the condition inside the lungs. Lungs vary in size, a larger man naturally having proportionately larger lungs. So, in medicine, we are less concerned with the size, or total capacity, of the lungs, than we are with how much of that capacity is usuable. This usable portion is called the vital capacity, and it is measured in the laboratory by the amount of air that can be exhaled in one deep breath.

In our tests we've found that a conditioned man's vital capacity is about 75 percent of his total lung capacity. Often, however, an otherwise deconditioned man may match this, so we look at one more test, the maximum minute volume. This is the amount of air that you can process during one minute of vigorous exercise, and this test usually separates the men from the boys. A conditioned man will force as much as 20 times his vital capacity through his lungs in one minute, while a deconditioned man might be hard pressed to force even 10 times through. He simply lacks the muscle and endurance strength to perform at any higher level.

In some before-and-after tests with our Lackland airmen,

we found that, with just six weeks of conditioning, we could lift their maximum minute volume from 10 times to as much as 20 times their vital capacity. The figures are both an indictment and an argument. The airmen were just teenagers, yet they could ventilate just 10 times their usable lung volume in one minute. What could they have been doing all their lives to get so deconditioned so soon? But, so goes my argument, after just a month and a half of conditioning, they bounced back to top health.

After your usable lung volume has been measured, the remainder of the air in your lungs is called the residual volume. This volume is fixed, and even a conditioned man can't breathe it in or out. The lungs of a newborn child, for instance, if it takes only one breath of air, would float on water, because the residual air in its lungs could not be exhaled. This test is used at times to determine whether the child was stillborn or had lived for a short time.

However, too much residual volume is unhealthy. If your body deteriorates from inactivity or disease, the unusable portion of the lungs may increase, blocking off more and more space and making less and less available for normal breathing, let alone vigorous exercise. Ultimately, shortness of breath results from even slight activity, like climbing a flight of stairs.

So, if you allow your body to deteriorate, you'll be living your life with two handicaps in the lungs alone. When you need more oxygen in a hurry, the muscles controlling the lungs will not be in condition to force high volumes of air through them, and the usable space within the lungs may be seriously reduced.

The training effect can reverse both trends, exercising the muscles surrounding your lungs, increasing their strength and efficiency, and helping to open up more usable lung space, increasing your vital capacity and reducing the residual volume. In each instance, it makes your lungs more efficient organs to process more air and extract more of the essential oxygen.

THE BLOOD

From the lungs, the oxygen goes directly into the blood stream, your body's assembly line.

Here's how it works. Your lungs contain millions of tiny air sacs, called alveoli, around which the blood flows. These sacs are something like toy balloons, filled with air and dangling in the liquid of your blood stream. The air, as you've just seen, is forced into these sacs by atmospheric pressure. Then, following the Law of Gaseous Diffusion, the oxygen moves from the area of higher pressure in the alveoli to the red-blood cells where the pressure is lower (the red-blood cells, remember, are now in effect "empty bottles," having delivered their supply of oxygen and disposed of the returning wastes).

What you need to remember about this is that the limiting factors here include the number of red-blood cells and the amount of hemoglobin they carry. Even if your lungs could process more oxygen, your body tissue still would not receive more unless there were more "bottles" to put it in for delivery.

This is the role of the training effect. It produces more blood, specifically more hemoglobin which carries the oxygen, more red-blood cells which carry the hemoglobin, more blood plasma which carries the red-blood cells, and consequently more total blood volume. In our laboratory and others, tests have repeatedly shown that men in good physical condition invariably have a larger blood supply than deconditioned men of comparable size. An average-size man may increase his blood volume by nearly a quart in response to aerobic conditioning. And, of this amount, the red cells may increase proportionately more.

All of which means that there are now more "bottles" not only to deliver the oxygen, but more "empties" to carry away the wastes. The removal of carbon dioxide and other waste products is just as important in reducing fatigue and increasing endurance as the production of energy. It's like your own home. Even if you keep good food around, you still have to clean out the garbage regularly if you expect to keep living there.

When the "bottles" get to the tissue level, and unload the oxygen and pick up the wastes from the tissue cells, the process by which they do it is described by that old word we all had so much fun with in Biology I in high school—osmosis. The oxygen and food particles, now in liquid form, pass through the cell membrane—in one of the great wonders of life—and waste products pass out in the opposite direction.

That is the whole life cycle right there, materials for nourishment and energy going in and the left-over wastes going out.

To complete the cycle, when the carbon-dioxide wastes, carried away in the blood stream via the veins, reach the lungs, the Law of Gaseous Diffusion now works in reverse. The pressure of the carbon dioxide in the veins is higher, so it passes freely into the alveoli and is exhaled with the expired air.

The efficiency of this cycle, and its capacity, is a function of the training effect. Increase its work load and it increases its efficiency. Sit around and do nothing, and it deteriorates. It's as simple as that.

THE BLOOD VESSELS

The benefits begin to snowball. As the volume of blood increases, so does the blood supply to the muscles.

This improved blood flow, or tissue vascularization, is probably the most remarkable phenomenon of the training effect. It's as if our dairy had improved its regular routes of delivery, expanding them into superhighways, and opened up newer and smaller routes into the boondocks.

The improvement in existing blood vessels can have a beneficial effect on your blood pressure. If you've ever had a physical examination, you're probably familiar with the routine of the doctor rolling up your sleeve, wrapping a cloth cuff around your arm, then pumping air into it. The cuff is a sphygmomanometer, and the readings from its dial usually end up something like 120/80.

The figures, of course, are your blood pressure. The top figure is the systolic pressure, or the pressure of the blood against the walls of the arteries when the heart is ejecting more blood into the system. The lower figure is the diastolic pressure, or the pressure during the relaxed phase of the pumping cycle. In other words, the two figures represent the maximum and minimum pressures inside the blood vessels.

In a conditioned man, these figures are usually lower because the blood vessels become more pliable (i.e., change their tone) and the resistance to blood flow decreases. In a deconditioned body, both figures are relatively higher because the arteries tend to lose their elasticity and the resistance to blood flow increases.

This is all with the body at rest and the heart beating at a normal rate. Physical activity, and even emotional stress, since it raises the heart rate, also raises the blood pressure because the heart is pumping more blood into the system and at a faster rate. It can cause trouble.

In our treadmill tests, conditioned men would start with a diastolic pressure of 70, for instance, increase only slightly during their run, then return to normal within a few minutes. Deconditioned men, however, and especially the overweight types, might start with a diastolic pressure of 90, which is pretty high for a low-side pressure, then shoot up to 105 during exercise, and take 10 minutes or more to recover.

Many of our Poopers, especially those with clinical conditions, reduced their blood pressure significantly during their exercise programs. The blood vessels, because of the workouts they were getting regularly, made those beautiful adjustments that many of the body systems do in response to the training effect.

Years ago, the usual treatment for high blood pressure was "rest and relaxation," because the hypertension was, and is, commonly associated with the stress of modern American living. Now, regular exercise has been shown to be an effective means of neutralizing these unavoidable daily stresses.

One of my Poopers, an especially nervous type, used to jump a foot when I'd call out to him as he passed my office on his way to the dressing room. Now, months later, his overly tense, anxious attitude is gone. He tries to take everything "in stride."

It's a chicken-and-egg thing. Did he relax because of the physical changes in his body, or were the physical changes because he learned to relax? I suspect it's a little of both.

The second effect of aerobic conditioning on the blood vessels—and the more remarkable of the two—is an augmented blood supply, i.e., opening up new routes to the boondocks.

One of the most famous and amusing tests done in this area was reported by a researcher who set a weight on the floor, tied a rope to it, ran the rope over a pulley fastened to the edge of a table, then sat on the other side of the table and looped the rope over the middle finger of his right hand. Then, in time to a metronome, he began lifting the weight.

The first time, and for many weeks thereafter, the best he could do was 25 lifts before his finger became fatigued. To expand the experiment, he had a mechanic in the building lift the weight occasionally, and the mechanic always beat him.

One day, about two months later, the researcher began his usual lifts, but found his finger wasn't tired at 25. He kept going and ultimately reached 100. He suspected what had happened, and brought the experiment to a rather unorthodox conclusion. He invited the mechanic in again and made a small bet that he could best him. The mechanic accepted and lost.

Such is life in a research laboratory—some of them, anyway.

What the researcher suspected, of course, was the vascularization of his finger muscles—more blood vessels had opened up, creating new routes for delivering more oxygen, and they apparently didn't open up one at a time but a network at a time.

There is other evidence to support this conclusion. We've seen some in this book. Men begin conditioning programs, agonize for months trying to get the oxygen where it's needed, then *boom!*, almost overnight, the exercise becomes relatively effortless. Athletes report similar "plateaus of progress," improving not only day by day, but in quantum jumps.

This vascularization is the most essential factor in building endurance and reducing fatigue in the skeletal muscles, saturating the tissue with oxygen and carrying away more wastes, and is an extremely vital factor in the health of the heart, the most important muscle of all. More or larger blood vessels supplying the heart tissue with energy-producing oxygen considerably reduces the chances of any cardiac failure. And even if a heart attack were to occur, the improved blood supply would help to keep the surrounding tissue healthy and improve chances for a speedy recovery.

There's one final problem involving the blood vessels—fat metabolism.

Metabolism is a big word with a reasonably simple meaning—it means change. We've already met one kind, energy metabolism. Foodstuffs, burned by oxygen, are changed into energy. Tissue metabolism is another. This is the process by which foodstuffs are changed to make new tissue.

Fat, of course, is one of the foodstuffs—proteins and carbohydrates are others—and fat is important because it is one of the major factors in the development of arteriosclerosis, especially the fat known as cholesterol. The crust found on the inner walls of arteries in arteriosclerosis (hardening of the arteries) contains large amounts of cholesterol.

Your body can tolerate and easily metabolize a moderate amount of fat, but overly high fat diets strain its metabolic capabilities. When this happens, fat circulates in the blood stream for prolonged periods following fatty meals, and the length of time it takes to get rid of it depends on your condition.

At some time during your life, I'm sure you've heard some friend, or even chance acquaintance, talk about the good old days, or even the old country, claiming that Dad and Mother who stayed on the farm, or relatives who never left Europe, were healthier than today's Americans. Several researchers I know of didn't settle for this idle chitchat, but studied the problem scientifically.

One studied more than 150 pairs of Irish brothers; in each case one of the brothers had emigrated to the States and the other had remained in Ireland. The brothers in Ireland, he found, ate more food—including more animal fat—than their American brothers, yet they weighed less, had lower blood cholesterols and much lower incidence of cardiovascular disease.

Another study involved the Masai tribe in Africa. These hunters ate an unusually high amount of animal fat daily— that's why they hunted—yet heart disease was almost non-existent and their cholesterol level was low and did not rise with age.

The third study involved Swiss dairy farmers, who consumed large amounts of fat products in milk and cheese daily, which is understandable, yet they, too, seemed to live active lives well into old age.

In all three studies, the conclusion was that the activity that was forced on these three isolated groups was a major factor in their health and longevity and in breaking down these potentially troublesome fats and minimizing them as a health hazard.

I participated in another test, a little more specific than these. Our group of volunteers included some well-conditioned men, some average and some admittedly in poor condition. We all fasted from the night before, to eliminate interference from other foods and on the morning of the test we each drank 1½ pints (three-fourths of a quart) of heavy cream, unwhipped whipping cream, and nothing else. Then, still without eating, we took blood counts every few hours to see how fast the fat was processed out of the blood stream. The conditioned subjects lowered their total fat to normal within four hours. Some of the deconditioned bodies took up to 10 hours, or more than twice as long.

This was all from one sitting. Multiply that by all the fat your body takes in three times daily and you can understand the job it has, especially if it's out of condition, to get rid of it. Some bodies don't make it, and problems become inevitable.

Ideally, healthy fat metabolism depends on a combination of a low-fat diet and aerobic exercises, but if you have to choose, concentrate on the exercise. A high-fat diet and aerobics, as the studies show, are preferable to a low-fat diet and no exercise.

The training effect, then, basically does three things for the blood vessels, enlarges them and makes them more pliable to pressure, increases their number for saturation coverage, and helps keep their linings clear of corrosive materials for speedier routes.

THE TISSUE

This is the end of the assembly line. This is where the oxygen is turned over to the consumer and the waste products are picked up for carting away.

There are all kinds of tissue in your body, including bone, muscle, nerve and so on, and the smallest unit in any of them is the individual cell. This is the ultimate consumer.

Each cell is like a small factory, with its own receiving and shipping facilities, storeroom and power plant for creating energy, heat and new protoplasm, the stuff of which all cells—and all living things—are made. As complicated as the body is, it's as simple as that. All the food you eat and all the oxygen you breathe is meant to service this one tiny little factory.

Whether you service it well or service it poorly depends to a large extent on whether you send it the proper proportions of food and oxygen on the assembly line. Unhappily, the ratio is usually too much food and not enough oxygen, so the food just stacks up in the storeroom, and lays there useless, because there is no requirement to burn it and, even if there were, it couldn't be burned in the power plant without oxygen.

That's about as simple as I can make it. So, when you're thinking of exercise, think that you're trying to pump enough oxygen around your body to fuel all those tiny little power plants, and burn all that stored food to keep all those factories in business.

Now, to come back up in size from the microscopic cell, a group of specialized cells together form tissue, such as bone, muscle and nerve; various tissues combine to form organs, such as the heart, lungs and stomach; and several organs and assorted parts combine to form systems, such as the pulmonary and cardiovascular systems. Two more of these systems, the digestive system and the muscular system, are worth discussing in relation to the training effect.

THE DIGESTIVE SYSTEM

Aerobic exercises, as we've seen, have a relaxing effect on the body generally. They also have a relaxing effect on the digestive system specifically.

The Jake LaPrestos and the Rusty Cortners, who had all the signs and symptoms of an ulcer, saw them improve through exercise. Some people, like these, have trouble letting off steam otherwise. I know, I'm one of them.

I've never had ulcers, but as a close friend once told me, "You're too tense, Ken. You ought to blow your top once in a while."

But I can't, and running is my tranquilizer. I carry a heavy work load, starting at 7 A.M. and working straight through, usually to 5 P.M., eating lunch at my desk. And almost every night I have to carry some of the data home, rarely retiring before midnight. And, as any man in any job knows, you can work from dawn to dusk some days, and still produce an absolute zero.

So I look forward to my 5 o'clock run. It relaxes me, and I've heard a few hundred others say the same. One of the noontime swimmers told me, "The mornings are rough sometimes, but I couldn't care less in the afternoons. It's like starting a new day. I even talk back to the boss around 4 o'clock."

It isn't all psychological, some of it's physical. Conditioned men generally produce less acid in their stomachs. Exercise has a soothing effect, reducing peak levels of hyperacidity and its discomforts. Without exercise, these hypertense types often rely on pseudo-relaxers, such as tranquilizing pills. They're a poor substitute.

There is another benefit. Exercise is a natural cathartic. It aids the muscles of the digestive tract in moving waste material and consequently increases the activity of the bowels. In fact—and this is rarely publicized—most distance runners have, at some time during their careers, had to stop running and head for the nearest latrine.

Exercise and regularity go together. This is an established fact, and anyone who exercises regularly is rarely irregular. This is especially important for elderly people who tend to become chronically constipated.

THE MUSCULAR SYSTEM

There are three types of muscles in your body, voluntary muscles which respond to an act of the will, such as your arm muscles when you reach over to turn that ever-loving television dial; involuntary muscles which act independently of the will, such as the muscles lining the blood vessels or digestive tract; and the cardiac muscle, the heart, which is a little of both, beating independently of the will, but still responsive to it in moments of emotional stress.

The involuntary muscles independent of the will are affected by aerobic conditioning, as we've seen in the discussions on the blood vessels and the digestive system, but not to the same extent as the voluntary, and the cardiac muscle we'll meet in a moment. What I'd like to discuss here are the voluntary muscles, or the skeletal muscles.

And we're back to the muscles that show, the slim waistlines and the large biceps and all that.

If there's any one group that has given me more trouble over the years than any other, it's the advocates of the body beautiful, male and female. They can't understand why they can't earn points for calisthenics, weight lifting, isometrics, and other exercises aimed directly at the muscles.

One of them, in fact, stood up in an audience once and shouted, "What are you, antimuscle or something?"

I'd like to repeat here, for him and for you, what I tried to emphasize earlier, i.e., that exercises aimed solely at the skeletal muscles are fine, *if they are done in addition to 30 points' worth of aerobic exercises aimed at the essential organs,* the heart and lungs.

If they are done instead of aerobic exercises, you've got the tail wagging the dog, building up unessential tissue at the expense of the essential systems that nourish them.

I'll tell you something else. While you can't benefit your basic health much by performing muscle exercises, you can benefit your muscles by performing basic-health exercises, aerobics. It's an inevitable byproduct.

You can hardly do any running without exercising your arms and legs. The same thing for swimming and most of the other basic aerobic exercises. There is a toughening up, a changing of fat tissue for lean tissue, in any 30-point program. But this is not the issue. The muscles, while they may not become any larger, are definitely becoming healthier.

Here's how. In any muscle-building program, like weight lifting, you are building thicker, knottier tissue that tends to push the existing blood vessels farther apart, without adding any new ones to service the "boondocks." Such tissue has more difficulty receiving oxygen from the supply routes and disposing of wastes. So such tissue tires more easily.

In an aerobic program, the tissue tends to grow longer and leaner, so more of its area is close to supply routes at all times, plus the fact that an aerobic program creates more supply routes anyway. If you are in good aerobic condition, there is hardly any part of your body that is not well supplied with blood vessels.

This is probably the major factor why conditioned men fatigue less easily, even at a desk job. Their assembly lines are in excellent condition, servicing more "factories" and fueling more "power plants."

There are other byproducts to aerobically conditioned muscles. Ray Bolger, who is still dancing in his 60s, is also a lifelong football buff and has some educated theories on the subject. Asked why the players of today are so much bigger, yet so much faster, than the players of twenty or thirty years ago, Ray said, "They condition themselves like dancers today. We develop elongated muscles for elasticity. The old tendency in football was to develop bulky muscles, but they caught on that size doesn't mean anything without speed. So they're doing exercises that guarantee speed and quickness, and the lumbering clods of the pioneer days are gone."

One university, in fact, uses ballet exercises at football practice.

Besides speed and grace, muscle tone is another byproduct. Tone is a word that is bandied about by muscle enthusiasts, but it has a medical meaning. It refers to a muscle's firmness, a partially contracted state, even when the muscle is not in use. Some elderly people particularly, whose muscles have grown weak, have muscles that seem to just hang from the bone. They've become flabby and fat-filled; and they tend to sag.

Muscle tone is a good indicator of general health. A conditioned man's muscles are usually taut and firm, and one of the most visible effects of aerobic conditioning is the increase in muscle tone of the entire body, especially in the muscles most used, the legs in running, the arms in swimming and so on.

To all these byproducts, I have to add one more—muscle strength. Although we've done no direct tests—strength versus strength—we've seen the results indirectly. The data from a group of 600 Lackland airmen showed that, at the beginning of training, of those that could run an eight-minute mile, 85 percent could also do the minimum calisthenic requirements, situps, pushups, and so on. At the end of training, 97 percent of the eight-minute milers could do the calisthenics. But, many more could do the calisthenics who could *not* run an eight-minute mile.

In other words, those who were aerobically fit were almost invariably muscularly fit as well, but those who were muscularly fit were not necessarily aerobically fit. This became a significant study to the Air Force. It meant, that for mass testing, a running test could be substituted for the time-consuming calisthenics, because if the airman could pass the running test there was an almost 100 percent chance he could pass the calisthenics as well.

I get confirmation on this from others occasionally. One businessman, who joined an urban health club, started out exercising his muscles.

"I thought that was the route to go," he told me. "I'd alternate between the sauna room and the gym, working out with the weights and pulleys. I never went near the swimming pool.

"Then I heard about your program and jumped into the pool and forgot about the gym. About a year later—and I was in pretty good shape by then—I went back to the gym just out of curiosity. I breezed through the whole loop, doing 25 repetitions on each of the different exercise devices. It used to be I'd do 15 or 20 and it would wear me out. And I hadn't been near them in a year. How about that?"

How about that?

And, now, if you understand a little more about your muscles and their relation to aerobics, I'd like to discuss the most important muscle of all, and with it close out the assembly line.

THE HEART

This is the magnificent engine that keeps the whole assembly line going. It takes oxygen filled blood from the lungs and pumps it throughout the body, and takes carbon dioxide filled blood back from the body and pumps it into the lungs.

It began its work before you were born, it is working now and it will continue to work until the day you die.

And what have you done for it? Have you tried to lessen its work load?

Ironically, the heart works faster and less efficiently when you give it little to do than it does when you make more demands on it. It is a remarkable engine. A conditioned man, who exercises regularly, will have a resting heart rate of about 60 beats per minute or less. A deconditioned man, who does not exercise may have a resting rate of about 80 or more.

Just for the moment, suppose that you were at complete rest for a full 24 hours. A comparison might go something like this.

Sixty per minute, times 60 minutes, equals 3600 beats per hour. Times 24 hours, equals 86,400 beats per day.

Eighty per minute, time 60 minutes, equals 4800 beats per hour. Times 24 hours, equals 115,200 beats per day.

So, even at complete rest, a deconditioned man who does not exercise his heart forces it to beat nearly 30,000 times more every day of his life. But no one is at complete rest 24 hours a day, and for ordinary activity, like getting up from a chair, walking across the room, climbing a flight of stairs, the deconditioned heart would beat proportionately faster than a conditioned heart for the same activity.

So, I ask you again, what have you done for your heart lately?

If you want to do something for it, you'll get results in two basic areas; those affecting the heart tissue and those affecting the work load, the heart rate.

The heart tissue is all muscle. So, unlike the lungs, the heart does its own work, unquestionably the most important work in the body. The health of its tissue depends on its size and how well it is supplied with blood vessels.

We discussed the size earlier when we talked about the "athlete's heart." I'd like to repeat some of it here. Basically, there are three different-sized hearts. A normal, but deconditioned, heart is relatively small and weak because, like any muscle that is not exercised properly, it wastes away somewhat.

An enlarged, unhealthy heart grew that way usually to compensate for some deficiency in the cardiovascular system, hypertension or some valvular deformity. Such enlarged hearts, however, are not as efficient as the hearts that grew large through training. Their interior volume, despite their exterior size, is not as large, so they can't pump as much blood with each stroke.

The "athlete's heart" is strong and healthy, is relatively large, and highly efficient, pumping more blood with each stroke and with less effort. It is beautifully resilient and, if you could see it, would be beautiful to watch. Like any great athlete, it does great things with effortless ease.

Vascularization plays a large role. The heart, for its own energy requirements, needs the same oxygen it is pumping around the body for the other muscles, and a healthy heart is characterized by a conspicuously favorable blood supply. In short, its tissue is saturated with healthy blood vessels.

It's like a lawn with built-in watering jets or like one watered with a small garden hose. The hose might water the entire lawn eventually but, during a hot spell, it might take too long and some of the lawn might burn up. If part of your heart "burned up" because it couldn't get enough sprinkling, it could mean a heart attack.

The other element in vascularization, the enlargement of the existing blood vessels, was best demonstrated by one of the finest athletes America has ever produced and one, I'm sure, you've never heard of. His name was Clarence DeMar, and during his lifetime he participated in more than 1000 long-distance races. He entered the 26-mile Boston Marathon 34 times, winning it seven times and finishing in the first 10 on 15 other occasions.

"Mr. Marathon" was a man who enjoyed running. He worked nights as a proofreader on a New England newspaper, operated a small farm and still found time to teach classes at a reformatory for boys, in addition to keeping in condition for his cross-country races.

Clarence ran his last race, a simple 10-mile affair, when he was 69. He died (of cancer) a year later, working up to two weeks before his death, and his family allowed an autopsy. His heart was a museum piece, but the most striking finding was the condition of the coronary arteries, the arteries that supply the heart muscle. They were two to three times normal size—real superhighways.

Some of our sedentary types not only don't have enlarged arteries, but the small ones they do have are clogged with debris which reduces the openings even more.

A healthy heart depends on healthy muscular tissue and healthy muscular tissue depends on its saturation with large healthy supply routes. This saturation coverage, this vascularization, is one of the most important benefits of the training effect, and is nowhere more evident, or more important, than it is in the heart.

The second factor that indicates the health of the heart is the heart rate. Conditioned hearts, as they grow larger and stronger, can beat more slowly because they're pumping more blood with each stroke. Nearly all of the great distance runners have had low heart rates. One of the first men to run the mile under four minutes was said to have a resting rate of 32 beats per minute. A marathon friend, who's in his 60s, had a resting rate of 36 when I checked him a few years ago. The average office worker, who's a lot younger, has one of about 75 or 80.

What's yours? Sit still for five minutes in front of a clock, then take your pulse and count the beats as you watch the sweep-second hand. If you're 80 beats or above, you're not in good condition. The first thing to do is to get up off that chair and get to work. You might save your heart some of those 20,000 to 30,000 extra beats you've forced on it every day.

It can be done. Dr. J. S. Skinner, formerly with the U.S. Public Health Service, enlisted a group of desk-bound executives, 35 to 55 years of age, and after a training program of six months, their resting rates dropped an average of 10 beats.

These are all resting rates. Training also reduces maximum heart rates, which is just as important. Healthy hearts will peak out at 190 beats per minute or less, and without strain, while poorly conditioned hearts may go as high as 220 beats or more during exhausting activity, which is dangerously high.

We've put people on our treadmill, measured their performance, and found that those with conditioned hearts can literally do twice as much work—run twice as fast or twice as long—and with a lower heart rate than those with deconditioned hearts. Some supremely conditioned athletes, like distance-runner Peter Snell, have been run to exhaustion on treadmills, yet their heart rates never exceeded 165 to 170 beats per minute.

What lower heart rates really mean, then, is that at rest the heart is conserving energy (saving at least 15,000 beats per day), and that during activity it has built-in protection against beating too fast and suffering strain or worse.

Finally, training can condition the heart not only to reduce its maximum rate, but also strengthen it so that it can hold near-maximum rates for longer periods before fatigue sets in. Some of the Gemini astronauts, remember, ran heart rates of around 170 during their exhausting extra-vehicular activity. And I can't leave out the Scandinavians. Those Norwegian cross-country skiers have been known to hold heart rates of up to 170 for as much as 2½ hours.

I could hardly recommend that for your conditioning program, but the point should be clear. As your heart grows strong in response to training, it takes more to tire it. It will be quite noticeable. The first few weeks, or even months, of exercising regularly will tire you each time. Eventually, however, there comes a time when you are getting all the exercise you need (30 points!) without feeling it.

Smugness follows.

There's another heart rate that has nothing to do with physical exercise. In medicine, we call it the anticipatory rate or tension rate. You might want to think of it as the emotional heart rate. The telephone rings unexpectedly in the middle of the night, and you can almost hear your heart pound as you rush to answer it. You're due for a promotion that doesn't come, and you get worked up just thinking about it. All of these things, and many more of life's little crises, affect the heart; but training can reduce this effect.

It's this response to mental as well as to physical stimuli that makes the heart such a unique muscle. What happens is that two systems in your body prepare you for "fight or flight," starting the heart pumping to rush more oxygen around before you've even made a move. In periods of acute emotional stress, the sympathetic nervous system—an automatic system that speeds up most of the body's activities—combines with the output of the adrenal glands to produce a high level of hormones in the blood, which, when they reach the heart, cause it to increase in rate and strength of contracture.

Ordinarily, this can be good, helping the heart to pump enough blood to do whatever work the emergency called for. It's one reason athletes can put that extra effort into a performance, reaching down for extra reserves to "do or die for Old Siwash High." And, ordinarily, a companion system, the parasympathetic nervous system, acts as a damper to keep the hormone effect down below a safe level. It's as though the sympathetic system were telling your heart to "Go, man," while the parasympathetic system were telling it to "Take it easy, pal, take it easy!"

However, with deconditioned hearts the slowing down sometimes doesn't happen and the heart takes off, beating at an excessively fast rate, possibly leading to a heart attack. With conditioned hearts, there's a better balance, and you can "Go, man, go!" but still control it before you go too far. A high, potentially damaging level of hormones is simply never reached.

This, too, is part of the training effect. A conditioned body is less affected by these hormones, possibly due to more efficient utilization or to decreased production. Add to this the fact that a conditioned man's heart is already trained to level off at a relatively low maximum rate, and he has a built-in degree of protection against uncontrollable emotional crises. A deconditioned man doesn't have this protection. And if he's also a hyperreactor, a person who gets overly excited even in minor emergencies, then he has two strikes against him, too much emotion and too little built-in physical protection.

So the training effect benefits the heart in several ways, developing it into a strong, healthy muscle that works more effortlessly either during moments of relaxation or moments of peak physical exertion, and by doing so maintains large reserves of power to handle whatever physical or emotional stress is imposed upon it.

If you haven't done anything for your heart lately, start now. Exercise it. It'll love you for it.

The spin-off from the training effect now becomes a little subjective, and these things are hard to measure. But the effects are genuine, nevertheless.

SLEEP

You're probably my best witness on this subject.

If you aren't one of them yourself, you've probably known one of each kind—the active person who sleeps less than most, yet is wide awake all day, and the inactive type who can stay in bed 10 hours and still feel listless the next day.

We studied this phenomenon in one of our bed-rest programs. The two groups stayed in bed, flat on their backs, for three full weeks. One group exercised three times daily on bicycle ergometers strapped to the beds, the other group did nothing.

The exercise group had normal sleep patterns, sleeping their normal eight hours at the normal time of night. The group that did nothing slept erratically or developed chronic insomnia. Some had problems with constipation.

This became a significant study. The Gemini astronauts, especially on the longer flights, slept fitfully. The inactivity involved in weightlessness, added to the normal deterioration that goes on during a weightless state, indicates that some form of exercise may be mandatory for astronauts on long space voyages. It should help them sleep better and keep them more alert when awake.

Back on earth, the same rules apply. If you sleep soundly, you're more wide awake during the day. The listless types are those who usually don't get all the benefits they should from sleep.

Most trained athletes I know sleep like dead men, and my

Poopers, without exception, said sounder sleep was the first physical reaction they had to their conditioning program.

"I drop off five minutes after I hit the sack," one told me, "and I'm wide awake again when the alarm rings." "I haven't yawned since I started running," another said.

There can't be much doubt that exercise is the common denominator. It relaxes your body, sleep comes easier, and you get more benefit from it in a shorter time.

PSYCHOLOGICAL EFFECT

If exercise benefits the body, it can do wonders for the mind. In every study done on this subject, ours and others, a definite relationship has been found between physical fitness and mental alertness and emotional stability.

In the first place, improved endurance performance makes the body less susceptible to fatigue, and consequently less likely to commit errors, mental or physical. Your performance, whatever your job, can be sustained longer without the necessity for frequent breaks.

Russia is much more sophisticated in this area than American business or industry. Over there, when a man's productivity slows down, they send him to a reconditioning camp for a few weeks and it invariably improves his output. Russia has over 2000 of these camps. We don't have even one. In fact, I understand some American businesses take the opposite approach, training three men to fill one top executive slot. The morbidity and mortality rates among executives are so high that training more than one is always necessary. What a waste!

A study by Dr. Lloyd Appleton and Colonel Frank J. Kobes at the United States Military Academy at West Point made a direct comparison between the physical aptitude of cadets and their success at the Academy. They found that those who scored low on their physical performance test as entering freshmen had an attrition rate during the next four years that was twice as high as their classmates'. The dropout rate was especially high among nonathletes, those who had never participated in sports or exercise of any kind during their formative years. Without the benefit of physical activity when they were growing up, they encountered extreme difficulty in absorbing the training at West Point.

In addition, some of those in the lowest physical-fitness category on entrance failed to adjust emotionally to the West Point environment during their subsequent training. Colonel Kobes also found a relationship between athletic ability prior to entrance and later leadership potential.

A recent study on students at the Squadron Officers' School showed a positive correlation between performance on the 12-minute test and academic and leadership qualities. In other words, a commanding officer, if he wanted to, could stand at the 1½ mile mark and just about pick off his best students and best officers as they came running by. The others would be straggling behind.

These studies just about destroy the old myth that athletes are apes. Certainly some outstanding athletes, born with natural physical talent, are not mental giants. But there are only a few outstanding athletes. This is not the point. You don't have to be an outstanding athlete to be in outstanding physical condition. And the studies indicate that those who were intelligent enough to keep themselves in good physical condition were also intelligent enough to make it as students and officers.

And it's generally true in other fields, too. A man who is physically fit usually has a better outlook, a little more self-confidence, and often does well in whatever his talents and ambitions prompt him to try.

The training effect, in summary, is a cornucopia of healthful things for your body, with a spin-off of some peace of mind. At the risk of being overly repetitious, I'd like for the final time to review its benefits.

As I do, keep two things in mind. Forcing more oxygen through your body with aerobic exercises is what produces these effects in your bodily systems, and the total amount of oxygen that your body can process becomes, in turn, a measurement of the health of these systems.

The training effect helps your lungs operate more efficiently.

It enlarges your blood vessels, makes them more pliable and reduces the resistance to blood flow.

It increases your blood supply, especially the red-blood cells and hemoglobin.

It makes healthier body tissue, supplying it with more oxygen.

It does wonders for your heart, conditioning it as a strong, healthy muscle, relaxed and slow at rest, yet capable of accelerating to much higher work-loads without undue fatigue or strain.

It helps you eat better, digest better, and eliminate wastes better.

It helps you sleep better.

It may even make you feel better, mentally and emotionally.

None of this, as we have seen, is idle speculation. It's pretty well proven fact.

I like to think of the training effect as preventive medicine. It builds a bulwark in the body against most of the common cripplers, and you can start building this bulwark with as little as 10 points a week. By the time you've reached 30 points, your fortress should be built.

If you've started a little late, if one of the cripplers has already made its mark on you, the training effect can become curative medicine as well.

Let's now see how some of the others used it as such.

8: The Clinical Conditions

WHEN IT happened, Capt. Art Yarrington was 30 and anyone's image of a dashing young fighter pilot.

He had youth, he was ruggedly handsome, and he wore his flight cap at a rakish angle over a crew cut and a perpetual half smile on his face.

Art was a jet pilot, flying the supersonic F-104 *Starfighter*, one of the swiftest and most glamorous planes in the sky. He was good at his job—his commanding officer told me this —and he played his role well on the ground, just the type you'd expect to see as the cocky, carefree hero in a Hollywood version of the Air Force.

Then it happened.

"I was home that night," Art told me later, "and I felt this sensation in my chest. I didn't think too much about it since I'd been having some indigestion and heartburn, but still it was different. My chest felt full, and I felt like I should get up and exercise or something."

So he went down in the basement and did some pushups. "It didn't help, but the sensation went away after a while, and next morning it was gone. So I just forgot about it."

Typical. If I ignore it, it will go away.

But it didn't go away. As fate had it, lucky or not, Art was due for his annual flight physical just two days later, and there it was on his electrocardiogram: "Inverted T waves in leads II, III and a Vf, with curving of the ST segment. Diagnosis: Coronary insufficiency with inferior wall myocardial ischemia."

In Air Force language, it was a "serial change in an electrocardiogram" and in nearly every case an automatic cause for permanent grounding.

To Art Yarrington, it was the end of the world. After 2300 hours in the air, doing something he had dreamed of doing since childhood, flying the fastest and most-beautiful birds ever created, he was put out on the sidewalk, given a firm handshake, and told he would never climb into a cockpit of his own again.

"Isn't there anything I can do, Doc? Anything?"

Art was given a series of tests, none of which changed his status, but during one of which a flight surgeon mentioned our work at Wilford Hall. Art grabbed at it like a drowning man.

So about four months after the original symptoms, he arranged for two weeks of temporary duty, bringing his medical records and gym shoes with him. And he wasn't smiling when I first met him.

As I read his records, he sat with his hands clasped and his eyes staring at the floor.

"What do you think, Doc?"

"I think you have one chance in a million, but possibly it can be done."

Except for the history of an abnormal ECG, I saw nothing else wrong.

We ran our own tests on him (his ECG had returned to normal by then), and I asked him to give up smoking. Then we started him walking, first on the treadmill, then outdoors, slowly progressing up to one mile a day. At the end of the two weeks, he was walking up to two miles a day and some of his confidence had returned.

But I still had misgivings. It's easy to keep an eye on a man when you see him regularly, but Art had to return to his own base (for ground duty) and I wasn't sure I'd ever see him again or whether he'd ever persevere. We've lost others with strong reasons but weak wills.

When we said our goodbyes, I gave Art a program to follow, roughly a stretched-out Category I, starting with a slow mile, but working up to running as much of it as possible, and, when he could do it in nine minutes, to extend it to a mile and a half. The goal, through slow progression, was to work up to six miles within six months.

As we shook hands, I said, "Good luck."

Art winked and clapped me on the arm, "Thanks, Doc."

What I didn't know then was that, underneath his cocky attitude and carefree ways, Art Yarrington was a man of almost unbelieveable motivation.

All this was in May. Then, by letter and by telephone, I began hearing from him.

By July he was running three miles nonstop every day, averaging nearly eight minutes a mile.

By August he was up to four miles.

By September, it was five miles in 40 minutes.

In October, his average daily run was six miles in about 46 minutes.

He came back to Wilford Hall about that time for another checkup, all chest and elbows. "When do we start?" he asked, as he rounded the corner into my office, rubbing his hands.

We gave him a standard ECG, just to make sure (it was quite normal), then put him on the treadmill.

"What's your pleasure?" I asked him.

"The worst you got, Doc."

"All right, Sergeant Agee," I told the NCO in charge, "we'll test him on an endurance run."

Art snorted and started running. It started mildly enough, but we kept raising the speed and the incline, monitoring his ECG continuously. The worst of it was that there was no break. Art had to run nonstop.

We finally ran him to exhaustion, but not until he had been on there 15 minutes straight, and not before he had broken every existing record for our treadmill. He hit a maximum oxygen consumption of nearly 60 ml's/min, a figure less than one percent of the Air Force population tops, and he did it without going much over 180 heart beats per minute. Art Yarrington was in better condition than anyone I had ever examined.

After this demonstration, I thought it was time we tried for a waiver through Air Force channels to get Capt. Yarrington back on flying status.

The reply was perfunctory: "Recommend disapproval of waiver."

Art wasn't discouraged, and suggested something more drastic.

"Why don't I try for the Boston Marathon?"

My eyebrows shot up. Drastic, indeed! I had run in it twice while studying at Harvard, and it is a grueling race for a healthy man, let alone one coming back from a cardiac condition.

"I'm against it," I told him frankly.

But Art was adamant. The race gets newspaper coverage, and a story about an Air Force cardiac running 26 miles nonstop might raise a few eyebrows besides mine.

"Well, make sure you get yourself into condition for it," I ended lamely.

Art did. He increased his program to as much as 70 miles of running a week, and as long as three hours a day. By December, he was running 15 miles averaging nearly seven minutes a mile.

Then a minor tragedy struck. Art developed a foot infection that stopped his running altogether for three weeks. When it healed, it was too late for the race.

But Art was only momentarily discouraged. He snarled, "I'll show them."

Just to prove he could do it, to himself, if no one else, Art worked himself back into shape about a month later, marked off a track, and, with four fellow officers standing by as witnesses, he ran his own marathon, all 25 miles of it, in the respectable time of three hours and 58 minutes.

He was doing all this, remember, without any realistic hope that any of it was ever going to pay off other than by improving his health.

I used his marathon run as a basis for a second request for a waiver.

It, too, was denied.

Art dropped back to a daily run of from three to five miles, six times weekly, still hoping for a miracle. During this period I'd get to run with him from time to time, and it was with some pride and a lot of embarrassment. I'd set a pretty fast pace, and Art would match me stride for stride. About the three-quarter mark, however, he'd move in alongside and say, "If you don't mind, Ken, I'm going to run ahead."

Then he'd leap forward and, within minutes, he'd be out of sight.

Meanwhile, I thought I'd try one more avenue. I had heard that civilian insurance companies had changed from more conservative tradition and were now issuing policies at standard premiums to men with a history of chest pain if a coronary angiogram proved to be normal. This is a test which examines the coronary arteries from inside the vessels.

I requested approval from the Air Force's physical-standards section, citing this development, and their response was encouraging. So an angiogram was scheduled for Captain Yarrington at the Baylor Medical School in Houston, Texas.

The cardiologist there stuck a catheter (tube) in the large artery of Art's left arm and worked it up until it was very close to the heart. There he injected some special dye into the coronary artery and took moving X-ray pictures of the dye as it passed through the arteries supplying the heart. What he saw impressed him.

Among other things he reported, ". . . his coronary arteries appear to be larger than we would expect for the size of his heart and this may reflect his excellent physical status."

That's conservative medical talk for, "Amazing!"

The cardiologist asked Art how his arteries got that way.

Art cocked his head, "I run some."

There's an amusing climax to this meeting. When I called on him at Baylor to get the results, the nurse told me that, following the examination, the doctor was so impressed that he waited until dark, then went out in his gym clothes and tried to run a mile himself to find out what kind of condition *he* was in!

Now that I was armed with this favorable medical report, I tried one more time to request a waiver for Art's original abnormal electrocardiogram.

This time the request was granted.

So on October 17, 1966, almost two years after he was grounded, Captain Arthur Yarrington of Ridgefield Park, New Jersey, serial number AO-3029402, was returned to flying status after, in official language, a "history of abnormal electrocardiogram, possibly ischemic in nature but more likely the result of an inflammatory carditis."

Due to his accomplishment, Art Yarrington became something of a folk hero among his peers.

To understand the significance of his return to flying status, you have to appreciate the fierce independence—well within military discipline—of military pilots, especially fighter pilots. They love the Air Force, but they squirm under the restrictions of nameless, faceless sheets of paper that change their lives, when all they really want to do is deal with real people on the ground and fight some enemy in the sky. In Art's case, the enemy was some squiggles on an ECG chart and a form letter that told him, "According to Air Force Manual 160-1, Chapter 5, para 77d (7), dated, 3 Feb 64, you do not meet the criteria for flying Class II ..." with appropriate copies for all commands.

Art fought this, bucked tradition, and perhaps ushered in a whole new era in military medicine.

Don't be concerned that any of the men who run the Air Force might be upset about this. If the general officers I've talked to about it are any criteria, they're probably shaking their heads in admiration at his extraordinary achievement. The Art Yarringtons, remember, are the kind of men we send into combat. It's comforting to know that when his kind gets there and gets shot at, his chief reaction will likely be, "I'll show you, buster!"

And he probably will. Because, characteristically, Art's first official act after returning to flying status was to volunteer for combat duty in Viet-Nam.

Of all the rehabilitation cases I've worked with, I'd have to say that the Art Yarrington case is my favorite. Of all the chapters in this book, I'd have to say that I have the warmest regard for this one.

Don't read any hidden meanings into this, but it's something like the Biblical parable. Most doctors forget the 99 patients who needed only pink pills; but they never forget the one lost sheep who came back. This chapter is filled with lost sheep who made comebacks, and their one common denominator was motivation.

There are many medical limbos, some near and some far, but there is no route back from any of them without motivation.

I would like now to describe some of these limbos, and some of the routes back; but before doing so I should like to make one point crystal clear, in large capital letters.

Heart disease or any other ailment is infinite in its variety. No two cases are alike, and I would be guilty of gross malpractice if I laid down any hard and fast rules for the treatment of all of them. This field of exercise physiology as therapy for clinical conditions is still new, and there is still much to be learned. My own work in the field is only four years old, and the field itself is only 10 or 12 years old.

The clinical cases I have worked with, like Art Yarrington and the Poopers' Club, have—without exception—been brought along individually. The healthy but deconditioned Poopers had so-called textbook responses to the conditioning programs and point system. The clinical cases did not. Each of them, at some point during his program, had to depart from it.

The point I am belaboring is that, if you have a clinical condition, it would be foolhardy—perhaps fatal—to jump right into a program on your own. I am, of course, suggesting that you eventually get into some kind of a conditioning program; but I am also strongly advising that you get your doctor's approval first. He knows your individual case far better than I do. As it would be dangerous to exercise a broken arm until it had healed, it would be just as unwise not to exercise it after it had healed. Your doctor should be the judge in each case.

If you have a clinical condition, especially a heart condition, you *must* get his approval before beginning any program of exercise and his subsequent monitoring of your progress after you begin is mandatory.

If this much is understood, here is how some of the others fought their way back from the point of no return.

LUNG DISEASE

A good friend of mine, an overweight, inactive, two-pack-a-day smoker, suffered from obstructive lung disease, perhaps related to his overeating, underexercising, and oversmoking. Following an attack of pneumonia his condition grew worse until finally one lobe of his lung collapsed. (The lungs consist of five lobes, three on the right, two on the left.)

He stopped smoking, but the condition only stabilized. All the usual treatments were tried, including a tracheotomy through which an aerosol was insufflated into the lungs in an effort to reinflate the collapsed lobe, but all failed.

He stayed in the hospital for 10 weeks, but showed no improvement. In fact, he deteriorated.

Finally, he was discharged, with the lung still collapsed, and told to "take it easy."

But he didn't.

Being a doctor himself, he couldn't see spending the rest of his life with that kind of a handicap. So he devised his own reconditioning program. He worked up to it gradually until eventually he was running one mile five days a week, and playing enough badminton to fill up an hour. On the sixth day he played golf.

This went on for six months. When he finally went back for a checkup, the X-rays were negative, his lungs were normal, the collapsed lobe was fully inflated, and there was no sign of any abnormality.

This man was an extreme case, in both the condition and the response, but it's a fair example of a frightening trend. According to figures compiled by the American Medical Association, obstructive lung disease is the fastest growing cause of death in the United States. Bronchitis and emphysema, especially, are becoming diseases of almost epidemic proportions, multiplying more than eight times in the last decade.

Lung diseases are difficult to generalize about, because some of them overlap and it is hard to diagnose where one leaves off and the other begins. In fact, it often happens that one is the cause of the other. In general terms, however, these are some of the typical symptoms of each.

In asthma, pollutants in the air you breathe, including smog and cigarette smoke, or chronic allergy to ordinary elements in your environment like dust, may cause a mucous secretion in the bronchial tubes—the tubes leading from the breathing passages to the lungs—plugging them up in whole or in part and making breathing out more difficult. Your body doesn't get enough oxygen, so you breathe more rapidly, sometimes wheezing as you do.

In bronchitis, the bronchial tubes themselves become infected or inflamed, often following some other illness in the body, narrowing the air passages, thus slowing down the passage of air to the lungs.

In emphysema, the walls of the alveoli—those little toy balloons in your lungs—become stretched, often because of the strain from persistent or violent coughing, including the coughing of asthma and bronchitis. This over-stretching destroys their elasticity, and air begins to accumulate in them, especially in the areas less well supported by the muscles of the rib cage. As the air accumulates, the residual volume, or useless volume of the lungs, begins to rise, and the vital capacity, or working volume, is reduced.

In tuberculosis of the lungs (there are other kinds of tuberculosis), the lungs are infected by a microorganism. There is prolonged coughing, and often, if the lung tissue has been destroyed by the infection, the coughing produces blood. Tuberculosis has often been called the "poor man's disease," because it is usually associated with poverty and poor hygiene. Great strides have been made to combat it, especially in the development of drugs, but still, in the history of the world, more people have died of tuberculosis than any other form of infectious disease.

No doctor can diagnose all these illnesses on a mass basis, but I believe I can safely make some generalities. They show up more often among smokers than among nonsmokers, and some of these illnesses seem to be more common among the inactive. In the one case pollutants are deliberately introduced into the lungs and in the other the tissue is allowed to deteriorate.

When in each of these diseases the patient has some difficulty breathing, the traditional reaction is to "take it easy." He is advised to adapt his activity to the amount of oxygen his lungs can supply rather than to fight back and try to increase his activity and force his lungs to supply more oxygen.

One recent study by the Vocational Rehabilitation Administration showed that, contrary to the commonly accepted theory that asthma patients need to restrict their activities, two out of three of the subjects actually improved their maximum breathing capacity after participating in a supervised program of exercise.

Several doctors I know have started their lung patients into a gradual reconditioning program with encouraging success. After their condition has stabilized, the patients are strongly encouraged to get out of bed and start walking around the corridors, then up and down stairs. Some are given oxygen tanks on wheels or portable, strap-on oxygen containers and, breathing the oxygen, they walk around the hospital, and even outdoors where they perform nominal tasks around the hospital grounds.

Rest has been the traditional treatment for tuberculosis, yet at Fitzsimons Army Hospital patients with tuberculosis are taken out of bed when their fever subsides and put into reconditioning programs, even to the point of calisthenics and competitive athletics. The response has been very encouraging.

There are other lung problems besides these. The so-called straight-back syndrome is a condition where the subject is born with a spine so rigid that it pushes in on the lungs, reducing the total volume available for breathing. The old theory was that a low vital capacity meant restricted activity, yet in tests we conducted at Wilford Hall Hospital these straight-back types responded amazingly well to training, indicating that if they start with what they have and try to improve on it they can usually overcome their initial limitations.

Another problem is the so-called sticky-lung syndrome. This is the equivalent of an old toy balloon that has lain in disuse for some time. When you try to blow it up you find that the interior walls have stuck together, cutting down on the available airspace inside. Low-breathing types can develop this problem. The lungs, if not ventilated all the way to their periphery, may develop this sticky-lung problem, forming adhesions that stick together. However, these lungs can also be trained to open up, and it is highly advisable that they do. Otherwise, infections can occur in the unused portions.

Your lungs, the first processing station for your body's oxygen, need to be kept healthy by keeping pollutants out of them and by bringing more oxygen into them. Even if they have deteriorated, however, past the point of simple deconditioning, they can quite often be improved remarkably by an intelligent program of gradual exercise.

HEART DISEASE

Some figures, like the national debt, get so high and become so repetitive year after year that they begin to lose their meaning and finally cease to impress anyone.

We have that same problem in medicine. It's easier to talk about one or two cases, and describe what happened and what should have been done, than it is to deal in large statistics about exactly the same thing. No one listens.

But I'll try it here one more time, because the figures are frightening.

More than 14,000,000 Americans suffer some form of cardiovascular disease.

Almost 1,000,000 of them die of cardiovascular illnesses annually.

Cardiovascular deaths, in fact, account for 55 percent of all fatalities in the United States—*more than half!*

We lead the world in deaths from heart disease.

The United States, the greatest nation on earth, is a weak 18th in the longevity of its male population. The average man here dies during his 66th year on earth.

And the most alarming increases are in the number below 60, and even below 50. It's becoming more and more common to see men in their 30s with cardiac conditions.

The Air Force caught on and dropped the age requirement from 40 to 35 for mandatory electrocardiograms during annual physicals.

If all of this doesn't impress you, you may recognize yourself in one of the next few paragraphs.

The multi-factoral causes of heart disease, save one, are each old-American pastimes. The one, heredity, can't be controlled, but after that it's your own ball game to win or lose. The other four are the pressures of life in America, smoking, eating the wrong foods and too much of them and, the most popular hobby of all, sitting and doing nothing.

Heredity. Our parents endow us with a predilection for certain medical problems, including heart disease. None of us can control these inherited disease tendencies. Art Yarrington couldn't.

Art never knew his father well. He died at 27, and it's Art's understanding that it was a heart condition. One of Art's uncles also died young, in his 30s, perhaps for the same reason. So Art may have inherited a weak heart.

What can be done about it? What can anyone do in such circumstances? Just what Art did, face up to it! You've started life with one strike against you, and crying won't help, so face up to it and do something about it.

If there is a positive history of cardiacs in your family, you can assume you're cardiac prone. You need 30 points a week or more—even more than the person who inherits a good body and dissipates it. The tragedy in these cases is that, from the time you're old enough to understand, someone is always reminding you, "Your father died from overexertion. Take it easy."

So you take it easy and do less instead of more, allowing the heart muscle to waste away when it should be exercised the same as any weak muscle to make it stronger.

Stress. This is a problem that has been honed to a fine

point in America. There are two kinds of stress, acute and chronic, and they can be either physical or emotional or both. Acute is the more dangerous of the two. It could mean sudden death.

Let me give you an example. Suppose all those things we spoke of in the training effect never happened. Suppose you've allowed your body to deteriorate so that the lungs are conditioned to process only minimum amounts of air, the blood to carry minimum amounts of oxygen, the heart to pump minimum amounts of blood, and so on.

Now, it's a bright and lovely day, the birds are singing, the sun is shining, you're in a good mood, and this teenage jalopy comes tearing out of a side street and crashes into your car, spinning it around and smashing it into a lamp pole.

You aren't hurt, your safety belt was snugly in place, you haven't even moved from your seat. But your heart is beating like a triphammer. It could kill you right there, though you've hardly moved a muscle. Why?

It's emotional stress, of course, but do you really understand what goes on in your body during moments like this? We discussed this some in the last chapter, but let's carry it to the extreme.

It's a fight-or-flight moment, and your body—specifically the sympathetic nervous system—tries to accommodate the emotional emergency with a fresh supply of hormones to stimulate the heart to a higher work load. But, as we've just said, your heart is no longer in condition to take on this higher work load. Yet it is forced to pump blood through at a faster rate, and if the situation continues long enough, or the rate goes high enough, it could give up.

Heart attacks are not uncommon at moments like this. It's called a "sympathetic storm." The sympathetic system produces a rash of hormones, more than the parasympathetic system can neutralize and more than the heart can safely handle.

It's like a worn-out jet engine that's thrown into afterburner to get that extra boost of power from it. The engine could, and sometimes does, explode.

I've known several such cases in my own personal experience. Back when I was interning at King County Hospital in Seattle, Wash., I was called to a ward where a heart patient was having another attack. We screened the area off, but couldn't screen off the noise, so the rest of the ward pretty well knew what was going on. We worked on the patient for 45 minutes, with artificial respiration and heart massage, and finally succeeded.

When we had finished, I turned around, drew back the screen, and saw another woman across the aisle, an asthmatic, topple over in her bed. She was dead.

We had saved one, but lost another not even involved.

It was obviously a sympathetic storm. The woman was not that ill, physically. In fact, from her records, it was a question whether she should even have been admitted. It was just her emotional reaction to someone else's emergency that sent her deconditioned, but otherwise well, heart "over the top."

Right here in San Antonio, a uniformed policeman knocked on the door of a residence to inform a woman that her son had been killed in an automobile accident. The woman dropped dead at his feet. You've heard of "voodoo" deaths, where witch doctors scare people to death. It's medically possible. Sympathetic storms can do it.

These storms, however, do not have to be entirely emotional. Acute physical stress can produce the same result. An obvious example might be a holdup. Suppose it happens to you, and you start running and the gunman starts shooting. The emotions of the moment and the physical stress of running might be enough to drop you quicker than one of the bullets.

An acquaintance of mine, a 37-year-old Air Force officer who was not in top condition, went hunting in Big Bend National Park in Texas and shot a deer. When he tried to drag it a mile back to the car, he got only part way there. He was found alongside the deer, dead of a heart attack. An autopsy showed nothing wrong with his heart, but apparently a sympathetic storm had sent it "over the top."

One famous study on animals supports the conclusion that acute physical stress can affect the heart seriously. One set of animals was exercised regularly, the other was kept caged. Then all were subjected to acute physical stress, some to extreme cold, for instance, and so on. The conditioned animals survived all of it, while some of the deconditioned animals developed acute, severe cardiac problems.

The second kind of stress is chronic stress, often called the "Madison Avenue syndrome." While not as immediately dangerous as acute stress, its cumulative effect over a period of years can be just as deadly.

It's probably the most American of all heart problems because it often strikes the go-getters, the man who just has to get that $1-million account, make that big sale, get that big promotion, and it drives him his whole life long.

The chronic stress of trying to get ahead in the world stimulates the sympathetic nervous system and the adrenal system just as definitely as acute stress, though not to the same degree. Over a period of time, however, with a high level of hormones constantly in circulation, it can eventually cause isolated areas of fibrosis, or scars of the heart. If enough scars accumulate, they can interfere with the heart's electrical activity, destroy its tissue, and may subsequently stop it altogether.

A man with this problem, constantly on the go, ought to do some of his going on a track or in a swimming pool and help put a damper on his unwanted hormone stimulation.

Smoking. So much has been said and written lately about the poor cigarette, all of it bad, that it's probably time someone came out in favor of it, if only in sympathy for the underdog.

I'm afraid I'm not the man for the job.

Every medical study I've ever read on the subject condemns smoking, especially cigarettes, without any recommendation for mercy. Even the more conservative reports "put it at the scene of the crime."

The most recent government report found that more than 70 percent of the men who smoked two packs a day or more already had at least one chronic condition that impaired their health.

We've already discussed cigarettes and their effect on the lungs, but their effect on the heart can be just as hazardous. The nicotine in them has a toxic, or poisonous, effect on the heart by activating the sympathetic nervous system, again sending more hormones to the heart than it really needs, eventually causing scarring. Ironically, it's usually the men under chronic stress, the go-getters we just met, who smoke the most, using cigarettes as "tranquilizers" when actually they're putting their heart in double jeopardy, from the stress *and* the tobacco.

There are hundreds of reports on smoking, not one of

which comes to praise cigarettes and almost all of which would love to bury them, but one of the most famous is the classic Framingham study, which compiled data on more than 2200 men, from 30 to 62 years of age, over a period of eight years. Its major conclusion was that the heavy cigarette smokers suffered heart attacks three times more often than nonsmokers, cigar smokers, pipe smokers and even former cigarette smokers.

We ran some studies of our own on cigarettes, which I'll discuss in the next chapter, but let me leave you here with two comforting thoughts.

If you're a chain smoker, and decide to give it up, the toxic effects usually disappear within a few weeks, providing your smoking up to that point has not scarred the heart permanently. As the Framingham study suggested, former cigarette smokers are as well off as those who never smoked at all. The nonpermanent effects are transient. Paul Hibberd, one of our Poopers, dropped his 20-year habit of two-packs-a-day with no noticeable damage.

Secondly, several other studies show that, if you decide not to give up smoking, a vigorous conditioning program will probably reduce the harmful effects. Studies by the U.S. Public Health Service have indicated that heavy smokers can lower the risk of a heart attack with exercise. And remember those Swiss farmers with the high-fat diet. They're also heavy smokers, but they seem to live long, productive lives most likely due to their physical activity.

Diet. Unlike tobacco, something good can be said for food. The body needs it.

But, like tobacco, too much of it can be harmful, especially too much of the wrong kind.

Basically, too much of the wrong food—notably animal fats, dairy products, and sweets—does two things to your body. It clogs up the blood vessels with unwanted sludge and it adds more unnecessary body weight which these clogged-up vessels must service.

We discussed fat metabolism in the last chapter. Without exercise, a high level of fats is floating around in the blood vessels and, over a period of time, some of it starts interacting with the arterial walls, producing the so-called hardening of the arteries, or arteriosclerosis. The danger is that this hardened material narrows the walls, slowing down the flow of blood. It can also break off in flakes, called plaques, and float down to an even smaller vessel and plug it up. Clots can form around this plaque, blocking the vessel off altogether. If the clot is in a coronary artery, you've bought the farm.

However, even exercise, while it helps, isn't the final answer to the fat problem. It acts as a preventive, metabolizing the fats and helping to keep the level in the blood stream below a dangerous degree.

Exercise's chief role in this area, however, is vascularization, the creation of a multitude of routes so that, even if a plaque should break loose and clog a blood vessel, there would be enough routes to go around the stricken area and service the affected tissue before too much damage occurred. This, as we noted above, could be a matter of life and death if the affected tissue were the heart.

I would hold up for example again the Irish brothers, the Swiss farmers and the Masai hunters, all of whom ate generously of the wrong foods, but stayed active and had considerably fewer heart problems than their nonactive American counterparts.

So diet ends as it began, a lot like smoking. If you must eat, and everyone must, then exercise to dilute food's harmful effects. You might find, as some of our Poopers found, however, that a lot of food is no longer important once you get into a conditioning program and, what is important, you develop a taste for the right kinds of food.

"I have a ravenous appetite for fresh fruit now," one of my 40-year-olds told me, "especially the kind I can take a big juicy bite out of."

Amen.

Inactivity. This, in my personal opinion, is probably the biggest villain of all. Diet usually gets more publicity, but this should get the most.

A classic coronary-prone type is one who eats too much, smokes too much, worries too much, and does next to nothing. If his family has a positive history of cardiacs, then he'd better recruit six good friends and have them stand by for pallbearers.

Because the five elements—and statistics prove it—don't just add to one another, they tend to *multiply* one another.

My point, however, is that the hazards of the other four can be reduced with a conscientious program of vigorous exercise. You might say my advice is eat as much as you like, smoke as much as you like, worry as much as you like, and love your family whatever their shortcomings, but *exercise!*

This is an exaggeration, of course, but it has an element of truth. The reverse is definitely true. Without exercise, the other four could kill you.

Study after study has shown the therapeutic value of exercise. The most surprising thing about these studies is that the first significant one was completed less than 20 years ago. This was Dr. J. N. Morris' landmark study of several thousand London bus drivers and conductors, which dealt the "take it easy" school of thought its first shattering blow.

The drivers, of course, sat all day, so were assumed to be "conserving their energy," while the conductors who clambered up and down those old double deckers were assumed to be "wearing themselves out" all day long, their whole life long.

Yet, when the figures were in, the sitting drivers were found to suffer twice as many heart attacks as the active conductors.

Similar studies tumbled over one another after that, all with similar results.

Railroad section hands who worked on their feet all day were found to have less heart disease than railway clerks who sat in the office all day.

Postmen who walked their beats had less than postal clerks.

The same with factory workers over office workers.

Field hands over plantation overseers.

Farmers over townspeople.

Longshoremen over accountants.

Other facts emerged from all this. Even among the active types who suffered heart attacks, there were more recoveries and the recoveries were quicker than among sedentary types in the same circumstances. One study showed 47 percent of the inactive died within four weeks of their attacks, while among more active types deaths occurred in only 9 percent of the cases. Exercise not only helped prevent heart attacks, but reduced the severity of those that did occur.

Animal tests, done in laboratories under controlled conditions, produced similar results. Rats were made to swim, dogs were put on treadmills, ducks were stuffed with food then allowed to roam, while others of the same species were kept caged. In each case, the active animals stayed healthy and outlived their caged cousins, who frequently developed some cardiovascular ailment.

The value of exercise as a preventive seems so well documented that I'd rather dwell here on its curative value.

The classic animal study in this area was done by Dr. Richard W. Eckstein of Western Reserve University who, by surgery, narrowed the coronary arteries of more than 100 dogs, then divided them into two groups. One group ran four times daily on a 30-percent-grade treadmill, while the other group did nothing. The exercised dogs were constantly more alert than the listless do-nothings and, after four months of this, Eckstein reexamined the dogs to find out why. He discovered that the exercise had provided secondary pathways to the heart to go around the narrowed vessels, and suggested that "judicious use of early and continued physical exercise" could counterattack symptoms of coronary heart disease.

It becomes a question, then, of how much? Should you work up to a marathon distance as Art Yarrington did? Hardly. Art Yarrington is an exceptional human being who took exceptional measures for an exceptional purpose.

The standard measures, until recent years, were to take tranquilizers to reduce stress, stop smoking to eliminate harmful toxics, go on a low-fat, low-calorie diet to reduce the intake of plaque-producing cholesterol and weight-producing food, and "to take it easy."

Today, some of this has changed.

For the coronary-prone types, those who have not yet had a heart attack but are beginning to show danger signs, tranquilizers usually aren't necessary because a conditioning program has a more natural tranquilizing effect. The smoking ban still stands, however, and is getting stronger support all the time. A diet is still a necessity, especially for the overweight because, regardless of what else it can do, exercise alone can't take off any significant excess poundage.

But the days of the "take it easy" cures are long gone. They only compound the problem. The other measures alone are too passive, and just postpone trouble. Exercise is an active means of fighting back against trouble and possibly eliminating it.

Let's carry this one step further, to those who already have definite symptoms of heart disease, without an outright heart attack. These are the so-called angina types, the "pain in the chest" types. The blood vessels supplying their hearts are narrowed, cutting down the blood supply so even slight exertion can cause pain. Some of these men run heart rates of 140 beats per minute or higher just walking, and eventually develop a cardiac neurosis, too scared to do anything even mildly strenuous.

One of the most famous and courageous studies in medical literature refuted this attitude brilliantly. It was undertaken by Dr. Albert Kattus of UCLA in his revolutionary "walk through" program for angina patients.

He enlisted volunteers and put them on a treadmill. His ground rules were that they would indicate to him degrees of pain by holding up their fingers. One finger meant the first sign of pain, two more severe, and so on, with four being the worst pain they could think of. Some, of course, developed severe pain and quit.

However, the significant thing was that, for some who didn't quit, their pains began within the first few minutes, grew steadily worse, reached a peak around 15 minutes, then, as they continued walking, the pain began to disappear. Some stayed on 45 minutes.

They had "walked through" their angina pain.

Kattus entered some of them in a conditioning program, starting out walking one and two miles a day, and working up to four miles. Within months, most showed definite improvement, some even to the extent of eliminating the pain altogether.

Similar programs by others, some using swimming instead of walking, showed similar rehabilitation of anginas.

The last extreme of heart disease, of course, is the out-and-out heart attack, the cases where there is not just pain but definite damage to the heart tissue. One of the outstanding rehabilitation programs for these cardiac cases, mentioned earlier, was undertaken by the Cleveland YMCA.

The program, begun by Y-director William Cumler, attracts cardiac victims sent there by their physicians. It begins gradually, but eventually works up to one full hour of activity, from three to five times a week, usually consisting of loosening-up calisthenics, 15 minutes of walking/running, and recreational volleyball.

Dr. Herman Hellerstein of Western Reserve requested and received permission to come in with instruments and monitor some of the participants, whose average age was close to 48 and most of whom were executives recovering from a typical occupational hazard.

He found that almost all showed a remarkable training effect. The most significant findings were that the resting heart rate in some had dropped as much as 20 beats per minute, the cholesterol level had fallen, circulation had improved, especially in the smaller blood vessels, and he postulates that the hormone stores in the heart had returned to normal.

The usual death rate of cardiacs is five per 100 per year. Among the Cleveland group, the rate was less than two per 100.

Again, I think the therapeutic value of exercise is well documented, and some cardiac cases have worked themselves back into outstanding physical condition, better than they had ever been in their lives.

However, as heart warming as some of these comebacks are, prevention is much the better game to play. If you're still healthy, but recognize yourself in one of the categories mentioned, you'd better start your prevention program now. The cure might come too late, and you'll end up as just one more statistic that no one else will pay any attention to.

CONGENITAL HEART DEFECTS

This is something worse than Art Yarrington inherited. It's not just a weak or damaged heart, but a deformed heart.

One of my Poopers had such a problem, a hole inside his heart called an atrial septal defect. Following an operation in which the surgeons repaired this defect, he seemed to grow weaker. The surgery was successful but he couldn't regain his strength. We started training him and before long he was running a mile in 7½ minutes and a mile and a half in 10½ minutes. Not bad for a man following open-heart surgery.

This was another example of a post-surgery case who responded very well to training. He tried "taking it easy" after his operation, and got worse. He began exercising and got better.

Many surgeons are now looking toward exercise as both pre-operative and post-operative care. Some use a treadmill test for their patients, both before and after open-heart surgery. It shows them, first, whether surgery is needed and whether the patient is in condition to survive it, and, second, how well the patient has responded to surgery.

Others use conditioning programs before operations for their patients so they can tolerate more in the operating room, and recover more quickly afterward. Strengthened muscles, improved return of the blood through the veins, more efficient respiration, and lower heart rates are among the benefits cited. In some cases, like Jake LaPresto, the need for an operation was postponed, apparently indefinitely.

This is a new trend in medicine, and it shows great promise.

HIGH BLOOD PRESSURE

My friend, Dr. Bruno Balke, once accepted a patient, a slightly overweight 53-year-old, whose blood pressure had steadily increased, despite treatment, over a period of three years. When he first came to Dr. Balke, his readings were 184/110 at rest, which is not healthy.

He was put into a conditioning program and, at the end of 12 weeks, as measured by oxygen-consumption tests and treadmill performance, his working capacity had increased by 25 percent. More significantly, his blood pressure had dropped to 140/90.

High blood pressure (hypertension) is a major problem in this country, affecting up to 15 percent of the adult population. Dr. Balke's success with his patient may not be duplicated in all cases, because there are many different and variable causes for hypertension and they do not always respond to the same treatment. I have always been very careful treating these cases.

Obesity is one factor frequently associated with high blood pressure, although the exact relationship between the two is still obscure.

In other cases it is associated with nervousness, which can also send the heart rate soaring, pumping more blood into the system than it is equipped for.

And in still other cases, it is associated with aging. Here the blood vessels themselves have aged, hardened and become less pliable, so that even normal blood flow raises the pressure within them.

The standard treatment is often weight reduction combined with medication, or just medication by itself.

The medication—drugs to reduce the pressure, lower the heart rate, or relieve anxiety—has had some success. However, at least one report published in the *Journal of the American Medical Association* showed no difference in survival between matched pairs, one set of patients who had been treated with medication and the other set who had not.

It has made some doctors, including myself, wonder about the efficacy of medication in mild cases of hypertension, and to look closely at exercise as therapy to whip the heart, the blood vessels, and the psyche itself back into shape. The training effect can, as we've seen, reduce the heart rate, which in itself tends to lower blood pressure; and it can relax the body, relieving tensions.

Other studies confirm this result. Dr. Fred Kasch of San Diego, Calif., put a group of over-50 types into a training program and their pressures went down from an average of 155/103 to an average of 144/94.

The lower figure, the diastolic pressure, is more important, especially in aging. It is a measurement of the elasticity of the arteries. If they harden, the pressure goes up. Diet can also be a factor in the early hardening of arteries.

If you're concerned about your own blood pressure, you might want to measure it against Air Force standards for flying status. Up to the age of 35, a reading of less than 140/90 is required; between 35 and 45, 150/90; and over 45, less than 154/94 is acceptable. The old rule of thumb, 100 plus your age, is still reasonably valid for your systolic pressure through middle age. It should not go much over 150, however, regardless of age. But, as I said, the lower figure is more important. The diastolic pressure tells you the amount of resistance to blood flow, not the ejection force of the heart.

If conditioning is a factor in the relief of high blood pressure, and I believe it is, it again becomes a question of how much conditioning is required.

Hellerstein's findings at Cleveland showed that a low-level program produced no significant reduction in blood pressure. Dr. Joseph Mastropaolo, formerly of Chicago, Ill., on the other hand, showed a significant drop in pressure in response to vigorous training. In our work, we've also seen a drop in blood pressure in all our Poopers who have maintained a 30-point week.

My recommendation: Work up to a 30-point week—under supervision. The training effect should then help to solve the pressure problem by natural means.

VARICOSE VEINS

If you haven't developed any respect for your heart by now, let me tell you something else about it.

The blood in your body could fall to your ankles when you stand, and stay there, by the force of gravity alone. Yet the heart not only pumps it all around the body, including the ankles, but it pumps with enough force to send it all the way back up again by way of the veins.

It gets some help from healthy blood vessels and muscles surrounding the veins which squeeze them to prevent pooling in the ankles during long hours on your feet. Remember the classic photo of the Buckingham Palace guard in his tall wooly hat keeled over on the parade ground while the Queen passes by? He had fainted, probably because the blood had pooled in his legs, robbing his brain—at the far end of his body—of its normal supply. Hence, unconsciousness.

If this pooling continues, even slightly, over a long period of years, varicose veins can appear. It's a condition usually associated with aging. There is a loss of tone in the veins. They can't maintain their elasticity, so they begin to sag and blood pools in the legs. It often shows up as blotchy areas around the ankles.

People who develop varicose veins are usually obese, inactive types, so exercise is more of a preventive than a cure for varicose veins. It keeps the muscles strong and the blood vessels healthy, decreasing the time the blood spends in the ankles.

Varicose veins are, truly, damaged blood vessels, so their cure is not as likely as if they were merely deconditioned. However, although there are no studies in this field, I'm convinced, based on the beneficial changes in the veins of deconditioned people, that a daily exercise program could make *some* of the same changes in varicose veins. The wife of one of our Poopers, who had a very painful case of varicose veins began running with her husband and within five weeks the pain disappeared. Unfortunately, she didn't continue exercising and the pain returned some two months later.

STOMACH ULCERS

After heart disease and high blood pressure, ulcers are the third most common cause for grounding Air Force pilots. Ulcer disease has always been a problem in the United States —in this land of the free and the home of the go-getter—and it seems to be getting worse.

Ulcers are directly related to environmental stress, with heredity compounding the problem. Some people are born worriers, and the stresses of life in America today—job stresses, family stresses—are no help at all.

Worriers, to put it in its simplest terms, produce too much acid in their stomachs, and this hyperacidity is one of the contributory causes of ulcers. It just eats away the lining of the stomach, or of the duodenum a little further down in the digestive tract. Unless stopped, it can come in contact with a blood vessel. Hence, bleeding ulcers.

The traditional methods of treating an ulcer are still valid. The patient must be calmed down, either by removing the stresses or convincing him that he must face them with greater equanimity. Either method will help reduce the production of excess acid. Then, he is put on a bland diet, so that whatever he eats will not aggravate his stomach any more; and he is given medication to neutralize the excess acid already present.

All of this presumes that the stomach, though in pain, is still intact. If, as in Ben Kartman's case, the acid has too much of a head start, an operation may be necessary to remove or sew up the damaged areas.

I suspect that some of these operations could have been avoided. Ulcers generally attack men in the upper levels of intelligence, men who are inclined to accept more responsibility than they can handle at the moment. Such men have pride, too much perhaps, and are more likely to treat stomach pain as indigestion rather than admit there is something more serious wrong with them. By the time the pain gets unbearable, and they finally take the doctor into their confidence, the condition is critical. So I suspect there are a lot more ulcer victims walking around than their doctors know about.

In working with them, we took the standard measures one step further, and not without precedent. In animal experiments, reported in Maxcy's text-book of *Preventive Medicine & Public Health,* dogs were injected with acid-producing medication, then some were run on treadmills to the point of exhaustion, while the others sat around in confinement. The confined animals developed ulcers, while the running animals did not.

Among our Poopers, Jake LaPresto had ulcer symptoms and Rusty Cortner was well on the way toward getting them, and they both ran away from them. I believe that exhaustive exercise and the resultant muscular fatigue either reduced the amount of stomach acid produced or neutralized it. The relaxing effect on the body, which is a universal reaction in men who enter a conditioning program, can be a major factor in preventing or relieving ulcers in those who are ulcer-prone.

If you're one of them, if you've had these recurring pains a few hours after meals, get your doctor's prescription first then his permission to start working off your anxieties.

DIABETES

We all eat sugar. In its refined—or better yet—natural form, it's one of the best energy foods, so we can hardly avoid it. And, if the body is in normal condition, the sugar is easily assimilated. If not, too much sugar can be dangerous.

Normally, the sugar you eat ends up in one of three ways. Some of it is used at the tissue level for energy—yes, sugar is one of the foodstuffs burned by oxygen to produce energy —some is converted into fat or other material and stored in the tissue—and the rest circulates in the blood stream. None of it is normally excreted in the urine. If you've ever taken a physical, you know the doctor usually asks for a specimen of your urine. Among other things, he's looking for sugar.

In other words, if you're healthy, all the sugar you eat is either used for energy, safely stored for future use, or kept at normal levels in the blood stream. It is kept at normal levels by insulin, a material produced in your pancreas. Insulin also circulates in your blood stream and converts excess sugar to fat. And fat, as we've seen, is metabolized by the body in another way.

In most cases of diabetes, the pancreas, for some unknown reason, fails to produce enough insulin, the balance is upset and the sugar begins running wild. I always think of Walt Disney's version of the "Sorcerer's Apprentice," where Mickey Mouse creates broomsticks to help him carry water but, once he has them created, the broomsticks run wild and he can't stop them and is soon inundated.

Diabetes, however, is by no means as amusing as Mickey Mouse to a diabetic. When his sugar starts running wild, two and three and more times over normal, he develops an excessive thirst, and an excessive appetite; he urinates excessively, and his urine is now saturated with sugar. If the condition gets worse, the patient's normal body processes can't continue and he falls into a diabetic coma.

Ironically, in spite of the advances made in the fight against diabetes, especially the discovery of oral insulin-releasing drugs, it's still a serious illness and deserves serious attention.

The standard treatment for diabetes includes insulin, to substitute for what the body isn't getting from the pancreas, a weight-reduction program to reduce the number of fat tissue cells, and a diabetic diet, which is basically a low-sugar diet to reduce the intake of sugar.

Again, we have no quarrel with this treatment. The diabetic diet, incidentally, is an excellent one. And I can recommend it for anyone, even a nondiabetic who is concerned about his eating habits. But we carried it one step further, to vigorous exercise.

Right here, I have to qualify this recommendation.

There are basically two types of diabetes, juvenile and adult. Juvenile diabetics must take their insulin in shots, and since exercise probably won't help them, it is not recommended as a type of therapy.

Adult diabetics take their medication orally to lower their blood sugar, if their condition is not too severe, or they take insulin in shots, if it has become serious. I can recommend exercise for both types, but with caution in the severe cases.

We've had most of our success with early diabetics, those not yet on shots. Many pilots with symptoms of early diabetes have been returned to flying status when a good diet, weight reduction and a good physical-conditioning program completely controlled their diabetes. (The beneficial effects of exercise as a method of controlling diabetes are probably all attributable to the conversion of fat into muscle.) This approach is especially effective with the early adult onset diabetic who presents with a history of increase in weight, eating the wrong foods, and doing little or no exercise.

If the diabetes progresses too far, and the subject finally has to take shots, it may be too late to make a major change in the management of his disease. But the amount of insulin required usually can be reduced with a conditioning program.

I would like to hope that, with further studies in this area, even the severe cases of diabetes can be controlled with a combination of insulin and exercise.

OBESITY

"Nobody can get along with a fat man."

"Fat men are jolly."

These are two of the most popular, and contradictory, misconceptions about the obese.

Know what an excessively overweight person is to a doctor? Sick.

Moderate to severe obesity is a clinical condition, the same as lung disease, heart disease and all the others. Even if it can be morally condemned as gluttony, to a doctor the result is a clinical condition that must be treated. The sad thing about it is that it seems to increase the likelihood that some of the other clinical conditions, such as heart disease, high blood pressure, kidney disease and diabetes, will develop.

In addition, studies show that the obese do not necessarily become depressed as much as the depressed become obese. The depressed often turn to food as an emotional outlet the way others turn to alcohol.

So the fat man is not as jolly as all that and, considering the abuse he takes from friends and relatives, and even the job discrimination he encounters, he is nowhere near as happy as the myth has it.

I want to make it clear early, even though I'm promoting exercise, that exercise alone will not take off weight. I'll repeat that. If you expect to lose weight solely through exercise, you've been grossly misled. Any of my Poopers, or anyone else anywhere, who has undertaken a conditioning program and lost weight, *also made a change in his eating habits.*

If you ran for a solid hour, covering 10 miles in that hour, or an average of six minutes per mile—and remember running is one of the most vigorous of all exercises—you would burn off the equivalent of about 1200 Calories. Then, when you finished, you could put most of it right back on again with a few candy bars. The average American, without *any* exercise let alone one hour of the most vigorous kind, consumes anywhere from 2000 to 4000 Calories a day.

I'm sorry, but anyone who tells you that you can lose weight with exercise alone is sadly mistaken.

Rusty Cortner, who lost 25 pounds from his 5-foot-5 frame, now eats only twice a day with a can of liquid diet food in between.

Jake LaPresto, who lost about 12 pounds, also cut out one meal.

Most of the others didn't lose any significant amount of excess poundage, but changed fat to lean and lost unwanted girth.

That New York writer, who with considerable difficulty swam his way back into condition, didn't lose an ounce.

"In fact, I'm more inclined to gain weight," he wrote me. "New York has too many good restaurants, and I have trouble passing them up. If my weight gets too high, though, say five pounds over normal, I just chug-a-lug a can of liquid diet for breakfast or lunch and eat heartily at dinner. As long as I know I'm in good shape otherwise, I'm happy just to keep my weight where it is."

This man is not obese, however. If you are, you're in trouble. It will get worse before it gets better, because obesity is a spawning ground for other ailments. And excuses won't help.

Dr. Jean Mayer of Harvard University's School of Public Health, claims that fat men are most adept at alibiing their condition.

• They claim they exercise, but examination shows they spend an hour on the volleyball court or in the swimming pool but only a small percentage of that time in actual activity.

• They claim everyone in their family is fat, which may be true, but their parents and grandparents didn't smoke two packs of cigarettes a day, and probably were much more active at home and at work, and didn't suffer the strain of modern urban life.

• They claim they eat only lean foods, but they eat them twice, three times, and more a day.

One study has shown that, even when the obese lose weight, they are disillusioned when they find that most of their difficulties, mainly mental, still persist. Obesity is much less a cause than a result. It requires a considerable amount of will power.

If you're obese, or tending in that direction, the best check is to start with the weight you had when you were in your early 20s. Presuming you were in good condition then, this should be your weight the rest of your life.

If you're 15 percent or more over that now, you're obese and you've got a problem.

And it's safe to say that Americans, generally, are grossly overweight. We lead the world, remember, in deaths from heart disease, and are well in the running in high blood pressure, kidney disease, and sugar diabetes; obesity is a predisposing factor.

Why?

As you gain weight, you add more body tissue that must be serviced. This puts added strain on your heart. Without exercise, it is deteriorating and you are giving it more work to do with every meal. Eventually, the strain becomes too much. Add one more statistic.

As you gain weight, fat is added which is not provided with a profuse blood supply. Without regular exercise, the vascularity becomes inadequate and the resistance to blood flow increases. Also, fatty deposits tend to build up in the vessels and the blood has trouble reaching the tissue. So the heart must beat faster and pump harder in order to supply the added tissue with blood. As a result, the blood pressure usually rises. High blood pressure is known to be a complication of obesity and a major cardiovascular problem.

As you gain weight, you become more prone to kidney disease. Kidney disease is probably the worst ailment suffered by the obese, but the specific nature of the relationship is still unknown. It's definitely true, however, that the incidence of kidney disease is higher among the overweight than among the normal. The kidneys, for some reason, begin to have difficulty excreting the body's waste products, which is their chief function.

As you gain weight, you add more body tissue, mostly fat. And fat tissue, as we've seen, stores sugar readily. Once the diabetic cycle begins, the body's insulin can't keep up with its requirements; and obesity tends to compound this problem.

What can be done about it?

Face up to it. Exercise alone won't do it, and diet alone is too passive. You'll cut down your weight, but you won't build up anything. You've got to do both. Basically it's a personal problem. Once you've made up your mind to that, I'll give you a tip that will help.

Know when Cortner and LaPresto and the others drink their one meal of liquid diet? Right after they run. Or to put it another way, they run just before their low-calorie meal.

Here's why. With the body at rest, you'll recall that the energy needs are primarily in the internal organs, the heart, the digestive system, and so on. So approximately 80 percent of the blood supply is going to these organs, with only 20 percent to the inactive skeletal muscles. But, as you move into action, the blood starts shifting to service these muscles with energy until, at maximum exertion, a complete shift has occurred with about 80 percent of the blood (and oxygen) going to the muscles.

After exercise, it takes some time, an hour or more, for the blood to shift back again. So the internal organs, during this period, are not being serviced maximally. To put it in layman's language, the digestive system is then in no mood to take on a lot of food.

That's the best time to feed it lightly, especially a liquid meal. You'll be slightly dehydrated after exercise, and your body will appreciate the liquid, and when your digestive system finally gets back all its blood supply, the quicky meal will have further killed your appetite.

Even if you don't use this method, dieting really isn't that much of a problem. The first day, like the first 100 years, is the hardest.

A good friend, who spent a week in the Air Force's Jungle Survival School in Panama, was dropped with his class into the Panamanian jungle with just the emergency rations ordinarily carried in a parachute survival kit. The rations consisted of about one cup of bouillon-type soup and one piece of jelly candy per day. The rest he had to scrounge from the jungle.

"The first day was unspeakable agony," he told me. "My

stomach was just one big ache. By the second and third day, however, it had shrunk so that the soup literally filled me up. By then we were catching animals—snakes and monkeys and such—and cooking them, but I really couldn't eat them."

My friend lost seven pounds in five days in the jungle, but this is an extreme case. Your case is well this side of jungle survival and certainly not as agonizing.

I could write a book on what type of diet to follow—and many have been written, not all of them good—but I won't do it here. I'll just give you a few quick hints, again with the advice that you get a more special diet from your own doctor for your own special case. Among other things, he can advise you whether supplementary vitamins are needed.

I can assure you of one thing, quicky diet fads won't do it. You've got to find a diet that you can live with from now on. Here are a few tips.

● Stay away from fats and sweets. Stick with lean meats, fish, fresh fruit and fresh (or frozen) vegetables.

● If you have a cholesterol problem, avoid whole milk or anything heavier, like cream. Drink skimmed milk or buttermilk.

● In cooking, use polyunsaturated oils or margarine rather than butter.

● Don't overdo it. If you exercise 30 points' worth, you must take in at least 1500 calories a day. The exercise will burn off up to 350 of it, for a net gain of up to 1250 calories for normal body energy needs. This is little enough to start the excess weight dropping noticeably.

It's worth the effort. The obese who come back, like Rusty Cortner, become doubly smug because it's a double victory. They've brought down the unnecessary flab and built up muscles.

In their case, it takes two to tango, diet *and* exercise. But it's a lovely dance when you've learned it.

BACK PAIN

"Oh, my aching back," is more often heard in the executive suite from the corpulent occupants of the plush leather upholstered chairs, than it is from those who move around more —and eat less.

Back pains run the whole gamut from simple strain to slipped discs. But they're usually associated with weakness in the muscles supporting the spine, and these muscles have usually been weakened by a shift in the center of gravity. The spine is now tilted backward to some degree because there's a pot tummy growing forward; and if the man tried to stand straight up and down he'd topple over.

Jumping right into a conditioning program might be a bit much for an inactive, paunch-carrying executive and, in good conscience, I can't recommend a running program without some qualification. Running may aggravate a bad back, in addition to bringing on ankle pains, so I would suggest walking, cycling or swimming as better starting points.

More important, however, the man with a bad back should begin a program of calisthenics to strengthen his back muscles. Specifically, situps where the knees are brought up to the chest are excellent for back pains, plus pushups. Others where the back is brought into play may be included, such as toe-touching or trunk circles. Working up to 20 repetitions of each of the 3 calisthenic exercises should be your goal.

The ultimate goal, of course, is a 30-point program of aerobics. But, if you start with calisthenics, or do them concurrently with your conditioning program, you'll have a better chance of success. You might also give some thought to dieting to get rid of that paunch.

ARTHRITIS

Pains in the joints can be even more severe than back pains, even incapacitating.

I wish I could offer more hope, but at the present state of medical knowledge exercise is more a preventive than a cure in arthritis. It is rare among those in a training program.

The two major types of arthritis are degenerative and rheumatoid. Degenerative arthritis mostly affects the over-50 types, and especially the overweight types. It usually affects the knees, the spine and the fingers, and can be the less severe of the two kinds of arthritis, although more common and less susceptible to exercise. The joints become painful, and when this stage has passed there is a bony type of joint enlargment and deformity.

Rheumatoid arthritis usually affects the under-40 type and any joint in his body. It is potentially more serious, but highly erratic. Severe cases can result in permanent crippling. Until recently, rest and drugs were the usual prescription. Lately, however, the American Medical Association has been recommending for certain cases a combination of rest and exercise, rest to reduce joint inflammation and exercise to maintain muscle strength and prevent the joints from freezing or becoming deformed.

I hesitate about recommending exercise as a routine treatment for arthritis since there are many cases in which activity may aggravate the disease. However, this area needs more study, considering the widespread affliction—there are more than twice as many arthritics as heart disease victims, and there are enough of *them* around. And when the evidence is in, I believe that, in selected cases, exercise will be among the recommendations.

GLAUCOMA

This is a silent, insidious problem that produces a visual impairment frequently terminating in blindness.

I studied the effect exercise has on patients with glaucoma, and the results were a pleasant surprise. I've also heard of individuals whose vision improved in response to an exercise program.

Ben Kartman is a case in point. When Ben first started his swimming program, he was, you'll recall, restricted to the shallow end of the pool because of his fear of deep water. If he wanted to read the clock at the far end he had to climb out and put on his glasses.

"One day, long after starting my program," he reports, "I was standing in the shallow end and glanced at the clock and this time I could read it. My swimming had improved my eyesight. I tell people about this but they pooh-pooh the idea."

I don't.

I suspect that Ben, and a lot of middle-aged and elderly people, have an insidious form of glaucoma—open-angle glaucoma—which creeps up on them and isn't discovered until it's too late.

Glaucoma is the No. 1 cause of blindness in the United

States today. About 45,000 people are blind on account of it, and another 150,000 have lost much of their vision from it. Still another 100,000 probably have it in the early stages and don't know it.

Of the two forms of glaucoma, infectious and open-angle (or noninfectious), open-angle is the more prevalent. What happens is that the pressure within the eye builds up, due either to excess production of fluid in the eyeball or because the drainage system becomes obstructed. In open-angle glaucoma we really don't know. However, the pressure build-up is usually slow and, consequently, unnoticed until the vision blurs. Blindness may follow. The victim's first clue comes when he sees rings around lights. Before that he assumes his increasingly poor vision is part of growing old.

The Air Force, obviously, is intensely interested in glaucoma. Nothing is more important to a pilot than his eyes. Until we ran our tests it had been assumed that exercise would only increase the pressure within the eyes because of the increase in blood pressure, so glaucoma and exercise were thought to be mutually exclusive. We found out differently.

The blood vessels servicing the eyes run right into the eyeballs. If the eyeball hardens due to the increased pressure in the fluid within the eye, an increase in the blood pressure in the vessels running through this fluid, so the theory went, would aggravate the problem by further increasing the pressure within the eye. So the standard treatment was to recommend rest, and apply medication to constrict the pupil and relieve the pressure.

The Air Force problem was that the medication, while it might help the eyes eventually, was reason enough for grounding. If kept up, the grounding might become permanent, and more highly trained pilots, and their experience, might be lost to the service.

In our tests, we took 19 subjects, including six with known cases of glaucoma, and put them on a treadmill, measuring the eye pressure before and after their runs. The blood pressure as expected, went up in all cases, and the eye pressure was expected to follow. *Instead, it went down.*

This finding was important since it indicated that exercise might be used as a method of treatment in some types of glaucoma. If successful, pilots could be returned to flying status without the need for disqualifying medication.

We also noticed that the men suffering from open-angle

glaucoma were deconditioned, obese, inactive, and had some abnormalities in their electrocardiograms, and a few showed early signs of diabetes. All were over 40.

It left me wondering whether glaucoma is an isolated condition, or whether it's just one more ailment suffered by the over-40 type who allows his body to decondition. If so, and if you're one of the under-40 types who have had glaucoma in your family and are beginning to worry about it, perhaps you can begin to do something to ward it off.

PSYCHOLOGICAL EFFECTS

I've mentioned this before but I'd like to discuss it again with more findings from Hellerstein's study with the Cleveland group.

These men, average age about 48, were mostly executives in the professional fields, earning $20,000 or more per year. They had been mostly inactive, and about a third of them were coronary types.

Doctor Hellerstein, before and after their conditioning programs, gave them a battery of the so-called "organization-man tests," psychological tests which ask the subject often-vague questions, the answers to which indicate his own opinion of himself. I understand some men have learned to cheat on these tests, especially when they're looking for work, but Hellerstein got honest answers from them once he assured them it was for their own good.

Before the conditioning program, he found they were very defensive in their attitude, often hysterical, very often depressed, and prone to high levels of psychosomatic complaints. In short, they were hypochondriacs, complaining about ailments that they brought on themselves or that didn't exist.

After conditioning, the depression began to leave them. Even the coronary cases became more optimistic, in spite of the fact that in the early stages there was still no actual physical improvement. The group, generally, developed a more positive insight into their problems. Their improved condition restored their self-image, rejuvenating their spirits, giving them a feeling of self-satisfaction and well-being and, more important, a better understanding of their disease and how they got it.

These documented findings confirm everything we've ever heard by word-of-mouth. A reconditioned man, especially one who has come back from a serious ailment, is a rejuvenated man in spirit as well as body. And it verifies that, just as the mind can psychosomatically impose ailments (like ulcers) on the body, the body can also impose ailments on the mind.

Exercise can be of value in relieving both.

* * *

If all of this sounds like exercise is Dr. Cooper's Magic Elixir to cure everything from snake bites to mothers-in-law, that's not my intention. It cures a lot of things, and helps others, but it's not the ultimate cure-all. There is no such thing.

We still haven't found answers to some ailments, from the common cold to cancer, and some men in excellent condition succumb to the very diseases I've been discussing here.

Clarence DeMar, who was surely one of the most superbly conditioned men America has ever known, died of cancer. A friend of mine, in good condition from regular tennis, died of a coronary attack. Another friend, a runner, ran in 100-degree heat one day, up a favorite hill he called "cardiac mountain," then sat under a tree to catch his breath. He was found dead under the tree.

These cases are the exception rather than the rule, because for everyone of these there are countless more who follow the rules and survive in good health. Even so, for those who followed the rules and succumbed, like Clarence DeMar, I can't help but feel that their superb conditions postponed for years, perhaps decades, something that might have occurred sooner.

Actually, I don't need these arguments. I have the figures. Men who live, not only long lives, but long, active and productive lives do it with the help of some form of regular physical activity.

If you're in this chapter and want to get out of it, or if you're not yet in it and want to stay out, then some form of regular physical exercise is necessary.

And a 30-point week of aerobics is the best anyone can offer you.

9: The Rules

ABOUT 4:30 or so every weekday afternoon the scene is the same in the corridor outside my office. I don't always recognize the voices, but the conversations are generally the same.

"Hey, fat boy! How come you're giving yourself 10 points? I beat you by a full 20 yards and I just barely made it in time."

"You were running on the sidewalk and cutting all the corners, buddy pal. You're supposed to run on the road."

"I didn't cut any corners. What difference does it make, anyway? You still didn't earn 10 points."

"Your watch is slow."

"Your head is screwed on backwards. Hey, Major! Do you see what this man is doing?"

About this time, I get up from my desk, close the door quietly, and sit down again, smiling.

Cooper's Poopers are coming in off the track, and it gets a bit noisy when they start marking up their wall charts.

One of the pleasant dividends of organizing a program among my own troops was the effect it had on morale. It's easy, of course, to get volunteers when you outrank most of them, but there was no real coercion. In fact, I bribed them.

About midway in our study, it got to the point where we had to try some of the data on real bodies. We work a 7:30 A.M.–4:15 P.M. shift, so when I asked for volunteers I offered anyone who would run and keep track of his progress a half-hour off from his regular work day. Most of them could then run at 3:45 P.M.

The first cries of anguish came from the section chiefs, who complained bitterly about taking men off the job for exercise.

"Why can't they run on their own time? We've got work to get out."

I soothed them down as best I could, hoping to get some results in before the work got too far behind. When the results did come in, the complaints stopped.

It was obvious that something unexpected had happened. Improved physical condition changed each man's attitude individually, but it also changed all of them collectively. Work production, instead of going down, went up markedly during their 7½ hours on duty. Their attitude toward their work became one of enthusiasm, and they were now getting more done in less time. And, in spite of the good-natured noise outside my door every afternoon, the so-called team spirit in my shop reached its highest level.

I offer this, for what it's worth, to any shop or office manager who's concerned about production and morale among his employees. Give them some time off and let them work off their tensions in physical activity, especially competitive activity.

The point charts are almost the focal point of our shop now. Early in the program, to cut down the noise, I took them down off the wall and started keeping track of the points in a book, and I nearly had a riot on my hands.

Everybody wanted to see who was getting the most points.

The final *coup de grace* came when some of the complaining section chiefs joined the program. I caught one of them lacing up his gym shoes one day. He shrugged. "If you can't beat 'em, join 'em."

When I'm asked about general training rules, one of the first questions is, "How do I get started?" My first rule is, join a group.

There's something about the American nature that is both gregarious and competitive. The typical American hates doing anything alone, and he'll do things in a group, especially exercise, that he wouldn't think of doing alone. Then, when he gets a friend involved in a game, the friend becomes the foe. It foments competition.

My Poopers run against the points on the wall charts—especially somebody else's points. The golfers have their handicaps and their weekend Nassau's. Handball and tennis players and others have their nickel and dime bets about who is going to do what and by how much.

Activity breeds competition and competition breeds more activity. I heartily recommend it.

If you've decided on a program of exercise, and are still dubious about how to get it started, the best advice I can give you is to join a program already in progress. If there is none, create one.

I always remember Airman Powlas' original decision, "I saw everybody else running, so I figured, 'Why not?' "

And Ben Kartman standing in the shallow end of the pool, waving to a dozen different people, and telling a friend, "This is my second home."

For group activities already established, perhaps the best place to look is your local YMCA. My respect for this organization is unbounded. They've been encouraging exercise —promoting health "of mind and body"—since before I was born, and long before my own medical profession got around to encouraging it.

The Y's "Run for your life" and "Swim for your life" programs are pure aerobics, and you'll be safely in an excellent point-getting program if you join either.

I've mentioned Bill Bowerman's Joggers' Club in Eugene, Ore. This is a good example of a created program and of the ground-swell of interest that was just waiting for someone to nudge it into action. Bill arranged his program so some of them could do their jogging—basically, alternating running and walking—at other tracks, or even in their homes and offices by running in place. Most, however, prefer to jog with the group. It's the nature of Americans to do so.

One man I know, who wanted to run but not alone, put a notice on the bulletin board of his apartment building explaining his intentions, and within a week he had five volunteers. They now run before breakfast in a nearby park.

Sometimes group activity isn't always possible. Some jobs aren't pliable enough to allow a man to meet with a group at a certain time on certain days. These men have to go their own lonely routes.

I remember one case vividly. A pilot who had been temporarily grounded for a borderline medical problem was advised to get into a conditioning program. I outlined a running program for him, but later I heard he had changed it drastically. I don't blame him.

He had been transferred to one of the Air Force's underground missile bases in the middle of nowhere. The crews live, sleep and work underground, 24 hours a day. No exercise is possible during this period; and sleep, because of the noise level from communications equipment and air-conditioning units, is fitful. And alerts are called periodically.

So after 24 hours of this, he was too bushed to run the next day, and the third day, after he returned to flying status, he flew. Then he went back underground and started the whole routine all over again.

He told me he had purchased a bicycle and switched to cycling to earn his points on his day off. It was less strenuous than running, and he could double up on it by using it for transportation as well.

This is a prime example of the flexibility of the point system. I would have preferred that he continue the running program, but his job requirements ruled it out. So he went to the point chart and found something that would fit his peculiar work schedule.

I would advise you to do the same. Groups are best, because they're a great source of encouragement. But if you're a loner for one reason or another, go to the point chart and work out your own 30-point week. It'll work regardless of how you put it together.

To help you put it together, I'll give you a sample point chart, similar to the wall charts we use for the Poopers' Club at Wilford Hall. The Poopers are all runners, so all that varies on their charts are the times and distances. However, to show you the flexibility of the system, I've included a few other exercises in a sample week:

Date	Exercise	Distance	Duration	Points	Cumulative Points
Monday	Running	1½ miles	11½ minutes	7½	7½
Tuesday	Handball		35 minutes	5	12½
Wednesday	Swimming	600 yards	10½ minutes	5	17½
Thursday	Cycling	5 miles	19 minutes	5	22½
Friday	Running	1½ miles	11½ minutes	7½	30

A chart like this can help you during your conditioning program, or when you're switching from one exercise to another. However, most men, once they establish a pattern of exercise can keep track of their points in their head: "Monday, two points walking from the train to the office, five points swimming, two points back to the station; Tuesday, four points walking . . ." and so on.

Unless you're in a group! Then, like the Poopers, you'll insist on public records publicly displayed. The Poopers dearly love to see how everybody else is doing, and they dearly love to let everybody else see how well they're doing.

There are some general training rules which I'd like to discuss briefly.

EQUIPMENT

This is not the obvious equipment, like golf clubs and tennis rackets, but the equipment in relation to health and hygiene.

Runners, for instance, can develop blisters. Comfortable, well-fitted shoes are therefore the first means of prevention, preferably with soft (not spiked) soles. I use a special pair of ripple-soled shoes—and a strong instep. Unless the shoe gives a little, while still supporting the instep, you can develop painful shin splints. The next way to prevent blisters, however, is the way most athletes do it, wearing two pairs of socks, a thin, ankle-hugging pair inside a thicker pair. The thin pair absorbs most of the friction rub from the shoe. If you still get blisters, clean the area, paint with an antiseptic, and cover with a gauze bandage and adhesive tape.

One word describes the remainder of your clothing, regardless of your activity—comfortable. It should be loose enough to permit the heat to escape and absorbent enough to allow heat loss through absorption of perspiration.

For distance running, I prefer loose-fitting jockey-type shorts rather than an athletic strap, because the strap or tight-fitting shorts can irritate the skin. If your clothes chafe, you might want to grease your body, especially the legs, before exercising.

Whatever clothes you wear, if you wear them regularly, wash them regularly, after every workout, if possible. That's just simple hygiene.

If you're susceptible to dermatophytosis, so-called "athlete's foot," ordinary hygiene is the best preventive. It's not nearly as contagious as was once thought, but some people are more prone to it than others. It can be irritating, even painful. Clean socks (white are preferable), clean shoes, regular bathing and airing of the feet, and, especially, toweling them dry after showering, particularly between the toes where fungi and bacteria can flourish. Talcum powder might help. However, if your feet do become infected, self-medication is not advisable. You're better off with some of the new drugs, which your doctor can prescribe for you.

One piece of exercise equipment, the bicycle, needs a brief mention. The points for cycling are based on American single-speed bicycles. If you're using a three-speed racing cycle use the highest gear as much as possible for collecting points.

TIME OF DAY

Exercising just before a meal, as I discussed in the last chapter, is an excellent way to combine exercise with diet. But wait at least two or two-and-a-half hours after a meal to exercise. Other than that you're on your own.

Some prefer "the first thing in the morning," especially those who don't like exercise. A big-city executive I know, who runs in a park before breakfast, snarled, "I like to get the darn thing over with, then I'm through for the day."

Another, slightly less disgruntled, told me, "It's a source of satisfaction to know I've done my duty, and I've got the rest of the day to myself."

Other men prefer the noon hour, especially the swimmers. It's the easiest way to fit exercise into their schedule. Others like the noon hour, "because it breaks up the day for me." Doctor Morrissey, one of my Poopers, doesn't run with the pack at four o'clock. He breaks loose from the hospital at noon and runs his two miles "so I can divide my day in half."

I prefer the five o'clock run. My work is done and the running works off any tensions that may have accumulated, then I've got a relaxed evening before me.

Art Yarrington prefers the "cool of the evening." If you're like Art, just a word of caution. Don't go to bed immediately after strenuous exercise. Give the body a chance to unwind gradually, at least an hour, before bringing it to a complete rest.

So the time of day is a matter of preference, and your own work schedule. All you really have to worry about is the time after your last meal and the time before bed.

TIMES PER WEEK

It should be at least three times per week, and preferably four. Some studies have shown that the training-effect benefits start reversing themselves, however mildly, with two or more days between exercise. Unless it's a very strenuous three days' worth of exercise, the days off could lose the benefits for you. You're safer with four, or you could include some daily walks to fill up the gaps in your more strenuous activities.

I see no reason to go seven days a week. The body needs some rest, if only one day a week.

WARMUPS, COOLDOWNS, AND CALISTHENICS

Spend 5-8 minutes warming up prior to participating in the aerobic activity of your choice. Some stretching calisthenics, slow jogging, walking, or stationary running are good. If you are running or walking long distances, you may prefer to incorporate the warmup into the early minutes of your run.

When you complete your aerobic workout, spend another 5-8 minutes cooling down by walking or jogging around very slowly. After vigorous exercise involving primarily the legs, most of the blood is pooled in the legs. It takes a few minutes for this blood to get back into the general circulation, and if you stand still or sit down during that period, you may faint. If you cannot stand, lie down, preferably with the legs higher than the head.

After running my daily three or four miles, I cool down with about five minutes of slow walking and then unwind with about 20 repetitions of some basic calisthenics. (As I've said before, I do calisthenics, I just don't count points for them!) The ones I prefer are situps with the knees in a bent position, some toe touches, and some pushups. Others prefer trunk circles or side-straddle hops, but as you grow older, the more vigorous calisthenics can be dangerous to the limbs.

Basically, calisthenics are good for maintaining muscle

strength and tone. Just use them *in addition to, not in place of,* one of the primary aerobic conditioning programs.

WEATHER

I personally hesitate to do any vigorous outdoor exercising when the temperature exceeds 98 degrees, especially if the humidity is high. If you're not in condition, overexertion in hot weather can be dangerous. However, if the workouts are mild enough, daily conditioning acclimatizes the body to the heat, reducing the chances of heat exhaustion or sunstroke. Usually, acclimatization takes about two weeks.

In cold weather, there are no restrictions as long as you are dressed warmly enough. However, if you work up a sweat taper off gradually. You'll be inviting a cold or worse if you cool off too fast.

Hot-weather exercise needs some additional discussion for another reason. The body loses large amounts of salt and water in hot weather. Extra salting of food or salt tablets (but not on an empty stomach) can solve the salt problem if taken with a lot of water.

Water can solve the water problem. The old idea that water should be withheld from an athlete is utter nonsense, dangerous, in fact. Just don't overdo the drinking of water at any one time.

There is some advantage to hot-weather exercise, however. It's called a synergistic effect. This is a doubling-up effect where a runner, for instance, would be getting an additional benefit from the heat as well as the run. The work is more exhausting in hot weather, because all the body systems have to work harder to produce the required energy and fight the heat at the same time.

Running in the thin air of higher altitudes has the same effect. The body is unable to get as much oxygen, so it works harder to utilize what is available.

When the superathlete of tomorrow is trained, he'll probably be trained at 10,000 feet altitude in 95-degree heat. Then when he returns to sea level, he'll probably run a three-minute thirty-second mile.

This is the reason many Olympic coaches are concerned about training their athletes at sea level, then holding the Olympics at places like Mexico City (7500 feet). The recent rash of victories by distance runners from Kenya is partly explained because these African athletes train at altitudes above 6000 feet, forcing their lungs and heart and the rest of their cardiovascular system to adjust to the thin air. Then, at sea level, they're superathletes.

For extremes of weather, I'd suggest reducing your program slightly, or exchanging it for something you can do more comfortably indoors. In hot weather, you'll get more benefit from less exercise anyway, or else you can switch to the "cool of the morning" or the "cool of the evening."

DIET

No one food will make an athlete out of you, regardless of what the advertisements tell you, but a little bit of all the good foods will help.

Keeping in mind the restrictions discussed earlier—easy on animal fats, dairy fats and sugar—an assortment of the following every day will give your body enough good food to work with: whole-wheat bread or whole grain cereal, lean meats, fish, non-fat dairy products, fresh fruits and fresh vegetables.

Variety should also include a balance between protein and carbohydrates. The old idea that athletes need steak three times a day doesn't have much support today. They need to balance it with "starchy" foods like potatoes or noodles or rice.

Several studies have shown the importance of a good breakfast as far as productivity is concerned, in the factory as well as in the field. It affects alertness as well as physical stamina, and the popular "coffee and a roll" just won't do it.

If you're concerned about food in relation to weight, most of the recommended foods run relatively low in Calories and most of the unrecommended foods, notably desserts, run high. A chocolate malt, for instance, would add about 500 Calories, which would require a half hour of running, covering five miles in that half hour, to remove again. Pies and cakes score high, as do fried meats and fat meats with gravies. Lean meats, fish (unless french-fried), vegetables and fruits score relatively low.

Alcohol, I'm afraid, scores high, and don't tell me about all the skinny alcoholics you've known. There are plenty of fat ones, too. More about alcohol in a moment.

SMOKING

We've discussed smoking in relation to health, I'd like now to discuss it in relation to performance.

I can remember our high school coach telling us that smoking was bad, that it might affect our health, that it would cut down on our performance, and so on. Most of us believed him, of course, without his explaining why it would do these things. Yet one of the group "snuck a smoke" every chance he got around the school, and chain smoked away from school. And he was a star athlete.

It was one of the inconsistencies of youth that none of us ever understood.

The chain smoker, when he left school, dissipated pretty quickly, but that's not the point. What I know now is that the coach was right, and all the coaches are right who tell their athletes that smoking is bad for them, even if they don't know why. Now I know why, and I'll explain it.

Let's go back to oxygen and the production of energy. Oxygen normally gets to the muscle tissue by way of the hemoglobin in the red-blood cells. You'll recall that the air we breathe is mostly oxygen, nitrogen and a few traces of other gases, including carbon monoxide. (Note this is carbon *mon*oxide, not carbon *di*oxide, the waste gas we exhale.) Carbon monoxide is a "bully boy" which confiscates hemoglobin much more readily than the "nice-guy" oxygen, literally eliminating whatever hemoglobin it gets hold of for carrying oxygen to the tissue. It's like our milk bottles were in a shooting gallery, and carbon monoxide was knocking them off so they couldn't carry oxygen.

This, as I said, goes on with the ordinary air we breathe, and ordinarily the effect is infinitesimal. But, start smoking and the effect skyrockets. A chain smoker, inhaling carbon monoxide with the smoke, can knock off as much as seven percent of his available hemoglobin, so that his performance is significantly impaired.

So my old coach was right, even in the case of the star athlete. He was a star because he had natural ability, *but he could have been that much better if he had not smoked.* Think what this seven percent might mean in most sports when some games are decided by inches or seconds.

So you're not an athlete and never intend to be. Smoking will still affect your performance. In addition to the things cigarettes can do to your health, they will cut down on your performance, limiting the condition you can get yourself in, in spite of the effort you put into it.

All of this medical theory was confirmed by one of our most significant studies.

We evaluated nearly 1000 young recruits at Lackland Air Force Base, and divided them into five groups, those who never smoked, those who smoked and quit, those who smoked an average of less than 10 cigarettes a day, those who smoked 10 to 30, and those who smoked 30 or more. Then we put them into the standard conditioning program.

At the beginning of training, only the never-smoked, as a group, made it into the good category on the 12-minute test. The stopped-smoking group was just slightly behind, and the other three groups, in nice, neat order, were three, four and five behind. This didn't surprise us.

What did surprise us was the way the groups started spreading out as training progressed. Their progress lines on the chart spread apart the way the peacock on television spreads its tail.

The 30-cigarettes group remained a poor fifth. Their performance at the end of training was only slightly above what it was when they started and still they were not in the good category. This left a significant gap between the fourth and the fifth groups.

All of the other four groups made it into the good category, still in the same order, with the next significant gap between the 10-cigarette group and the stopped-smoking group. The never-smoked, of course, were still comfortably in first place.

All of this, remember, involved nearly 1000 men, so we could hardly be in doubt about the results. I think it's especially significant because it was done on young men who could not have had many smoking years behind them. As the cigarette consumption increased, performance decreased. I can only believe that, as they add years, and more cigarette consumption, the performance gap will widen still more to say nothing of the health hazard to the heavy smoker.

I can only repeat, with as much emphasis as possible, smoking isn't good. It just doesn't have anything going for it.

ALCOHOL

I am often asked what is the best way to improve endurance performance, stop drinking or stop smoking? I would have to say, "Stop both!" The effect of cigarette smoking has already been discussed but alcohol also may affect performance, at least transiently.

Exercising with a hangover, or while still under the influence of liquor, will illustrate what I mean. Performance will be reduced, fatigue will be more rapid, and the effects will last up to 12 hours after drinking. These effects are at the opposite end of the assembly line from those associated with cigarette smoking.

Cigarettes prevent some of the hemoglobin from taking on any oxygen in the lungs. Alcohol prevents some of the hemoglobin from releasing oxygen at the tissue level.

Here's what happens normally. At the tissue level, the oxygen leaves the hemoglobin and gets to the tissue cells with the help of an enzyme system. Alcohol immobilizes these enzymes for up to 12 hours, so that the oxygen literally goes right on by. That's why alcohol dulls the senses and fatigues the body. The tissue—brain tissue, muscle tissue—isn't getting enough oxygen, so hypoxia sets in.

When I explained this to one of my Poopers, he said, "What you mean, Doc, is that the enzymes snuck off to the corner bar and got drunk when they should have been down at the receiving dock unloading the oxygen. Right?"

Right.

TEMPORARY HIATUS

Sometimes you can't keep up a 30-point week—in case of illness, for instance. What then?

It depends on the length of time off and the illness. The quickest way to find out is to run a 12-minute test and see where you finish, then go back into the conditioning program if you're below Category IV.

If the layoff is not lengthy, or the illness not serious, I wouldn't go through the whole 16 weeks again, but get back to 30 points as quickly as possible, immediately, in fact.

Obviously, I don't recommend too many layoffs, especially seasonal layoffs. Thirty points a week is it.

MENTAL ATTITUDE

As you've seen from some of the case histories, this is especially important at the beginning of a program when it all may seem pretty hopeless.

But so many others have made it and, if you don't have a severe clinical condition, there's no reason you can't make it, too. If you get discouraged, go back to a walking program but don't quit.

As you improve, and you will, you'll improve by plateaus. This is part of vascularization and the training effect. Don't expect day-to-day improvement, but rather jumps in improvement.

Remember, as much of an incentive as competition is, you're really not competing with anyone but yourself. The other guy isn't running or swimming or whatever with your body. You are, and it's up to you—not him—to get your body into condition, step by step.

Be prepared for "going stale," that period when you begin wondering why you ever started a training program. It happens to everyone. Just sweat it out. Go through the motions. Your enthusiasm will return.

Just don't give up.

The ugliest four-letter word in the American language is "quit."

Don't quit.

10: The Goal

PHYSICAL FITNESS is not only one of the most important keys to a healthy body, it is the basis of dynamic and creative intellectual activity. The relationship between the soundness of the body and the activities of mind is subtle and complex. Much is not yet understood. But we do know what the Greeks knew: That intelligence and skill can only function at the peak of their capacity when the body is healthy and strong; that hardy spirits and tough minds usually inhabit sound bodies. —PRESIDENT JOHN F. KENNEDY

That about sums it up.

From the ancient Greeks to the late President, leaders have been exhorting the multitudes to get healthy and stay healthy. And, I would guess, it was easier for the ancient Greeks to get results than it is for any contemporary leaders.

Like the song says, "It's summertime, and the living is easy."

Years ago, men were forced to get some kind of exercise just moving from one place to another. The sedentary life today is too easily sold, and the arguments against any exhortations from above have been too finely honed. "I don't have time for exercise," "Besides, I don't think it's so essential," and "Anyway, I don't enjoy it."

As a man who puts in a longer day at a desk than most, I can tell you that you can always find time for the essentials of life.

As a doctor who has specialized in the subject, I can assure you that exercise is essential.

And as one who enjoys life, including leisure, as much as anyone, I maintain exercise is one essential that not only helps you enjoy the life you have, but can help you to have more life to enjoy.

I'm not an ancient Greek nor a President of the United States, but I wish I could exhort multitudes, beginning with you.

What's to become of you, and all Americans—and America itself—if the present trend continues?

It's frightening and it's frustrating. Two million heart attacks every year! And so much of it is preventable! Even more frightening, it isn't getting any better, it's getting worse. Yet few listen.

In my position, I cannot help but feel that it's like the old joke about the farmer trying to argue with a mule. "You have to use a two-by-four to get his attention first."

I wish I had a two-by-four to get some attention. I wish I could somehow communicate what we've learned to everyone.

What is the ultimate goal of all our studies?

I'm not an anarchist, but I guess I'd like to start an aerobic revolution.

As a starter,

I'd like to see the basic fitness figures reversed. I'd like to see four out of five Americans in good aerobic condition, instead of vice versa.

I'd like to see tracks full of runners, pools full of swimmers, roads full of cyclists, trails full of hikers, courts full of handball, basketball and squash players. In fact, I'd like to see more tracks, pools, trails and courts.

I'd like to see fewer cars on the road and more people walking.

I'd like to see more people still as fresh at five o'clock in the afternoon as they were at 7 o'clock in the morning.

I'd like to see fewer middle-aged and elderly people, their faces flushed, climbing three steps, then pausing before attempting the next three.

I'd like to see fewer hospitals and rest homes for curing illnesses and disease, and more reconditioning centers for preventing illness and disease.

Yes, I'd like to see that day, when America has made one

more comeback, reversing the ultimate consequences of an affluent society and its inbred inactivity.

I'd like to see my country once again become a nation of doers instead of spectators.

I hope my own United States Air Force leads that revolution, but I hope, more so, that the rest of the nation follows.

I hope you're one of them.

Again, good luck.

Epilogue

IN SPITE of the progress that has been made in the field of exercise physiology, notably in the last decade, I'd be the first to admit that we still have a long way to go. Some of the studies to which I've made reference in this book are small and primarily suggestive. Many more and larger studies need to be done before conclusive and final data can be obtained. We've done a lot of work and we will continue but by ourselves we can only scratch the surface. Many years and many studies will be required before exercise can be given its proper place in the prevention and rehabilitation of disease in our society.

Exercise has been neglected too long, medically, economically and socially, and demands closer attention. To that end, I would like here to offer a few strictly personal comments.

First of all, some of my medical colleagues are still advising their patients to "take it easy," or, if they prescribe exercise at all, it's something vague, like, "Well, whatever you enjoy."

Frankly, I can't blame them too much. The field is new and expanding rapidly, and the average physician has trouble keeping abreast of the latest drugs and cures for illness and disease, let alone delving deeply into this aspect of preventive medicine.

It's time, however, that some concerted effort was made by the medical fraternity to bring all physicians up to date on some of the progress that has been made and to encourage and support additional studies.

Part of the problem was brought on by researchers like myself. We have not coordinated our activities closely enough so that some of the data we have collected—as important as some of it is—is not truly meaningful to the average physician, and to some extent to the researchers themselves.

Specifically, I think we should try to standardize our testing procedures so that the data from one laboratory could be matched point for point with data from another laboratory. Few of us use identical testing procedures. I'm as guilty as the rest. We've had to refine our procedures from time to time to gather data for our own peculiar needs.

It's difficult, for instance, to compare test results from maximum-oxygen-consumption runs on a treadmill and on a bicycle ergometer, or from level runs on a treadmill with runs where the speed and incline are gradually raised.

Each of these tests has specific worth, yet I still believe that some national or even international effort should be made to standardize some of the more basic tests, so the results would be meaningful for all. This would leave the more specialized tests—and we will always have them—for specialized purposes.

But this is an in-house problem, of interest only to my medical colleagues.

My more serious complaint is directed at the American attitude in general toward exercise. With the great majority of the population in a deconditioned state, something obviously is wrong.

We have some of the best medical facilities and minds in the world in America, yet one of the worst records of physical fitness. What a waste!

I think it's time Americans in general, and the leaders in particular, took a more sophisticated approach toward this situation. I hate holding up Europe as an example, again and again, but, let's face it, they're ahead of us in their overall approach to physical fitness.

I know we hold our own in the Olympics and in international meets among nations, but our athletes, you must realize, are from a small percentage of the population. The nation in general is not very fit. We've got to get off this All-American attitude toward a few superstars, and start looking more toward an all-Americans attitude.

In short, everybody ought to get into the act.

In Europe, as I've suggested earlier, they found that workers who became deconditioned fatigued easily. This affected their work output, even forcing some into early retirement. Thus production was lost in the first instance and the skills of the workers in the second. So the time and expense of training new men was added to production costs.

The sophisticated attitude, as I see it, is to do what the Europeans did. They set up reconditioning camps for such men, where they could spend four weeks or so getting themselves back into condition. The camps were co-sponsored, in some instances by the government, insurance companies and by the industries themselves.

The results paid off. The workers' production increased, there was less absenteeism from illness, and men stayed on the job longer before retirement.

What's wrong with doing the same thing here? The only thing wrong with it, as I can see, is that Americans generally hate being told what to do. My answer is that, left on their own as far as exercise is concerned, they've done next to nothing. And four out of five are good candidates for illness and disease, if they haven't already fallen victim.

And two million of them will go right on having heart attacks every year.

If sponsoring rehabilitation camps here sounds economically impractical, my argument is that I feel the camps would be self-supporting in terms of the economic benefits, greater production per man, less absenteeism, and a longer and more productive work life. I don't have any figures, obviously, because no such camps exist here, but some energetic economist might try to work some up on a theoretical basis. The government, the insurance companies and industry might want to sponsor such a project. It might be worth their while. In fact, some far-sighted management might want to give their workers 30 minutes off each day for exercise as we did at Wilford Hall.

Ultimately, however, it comes down to an individual decision, from the top executive to the average worker. Just how do you plan to treat your body? How do you expect it to serve you, if you won't give it the minimum amount of attention in terms of beneficial exercise?

I can answer a lot of your questions about the field of exercise physiology, but these answers I don't have.

Appendix: The Point System Expanded

RUNNING/WALKING

1.0 Mile

14:29—12:00 min.	2
11:59—10:00 min.	3
9:59— 8:00 min.	4
7:59— 6:30 min.	5
under 6:30 min.	6

3.5 Miles

50:44—42:00 min.	7
41:59—35:00 min.	10½
34:59—28:00 min.	14
27:59—22:45 min.	17½
under 22:45 min.	21

1.5 Miles

21:44—18:00 min.	3
17:59—15:00 min.	4½
14:59—12:00 min.	6
11:59— 9:45 min.	7½
under 9:45 min.	9

4.0 Miles

57:59—48:00 min.	8
47:59—40:00 min.	12
39:59—32:00 min.	16
31:59—26:00 min.	20
under 26:00 min.	24

2.0 Miles

28:59—24:00 min.	4
23:59—20:00 min.	6
19:59—16:00 min.	8
15:59—13:00 min.	10
under 13:00 min.	12

4.5 Miles

1 hr. 5:14 min.—54:00 min.	9
53:59—45:00 min.	13½
44:59—36:00 min.	18
35:59—29:15 min.	22½
under 29:15 min.	27

2.5 Miles

36:14—30:00 min.	5
29:59—25:00 min.	7½
24:59—20:00 min.	10
19:59—16:15 min.	12½
under 16:15 min.	15

5.0 Miles

1 hr. 12:29 min.—1 hr.	10
59:59—50:00 min.	15
49:59—40:00 min.	20
39:59—32:30 min.	25
under 32:30 min.	30

3.0 Miles

43:29—36:00 min.	6
35:59—30:00 min.	9
29:59—24:00 min.	12
23:59—19:30 min.	15
under 19:30 min.	18

5.5 Miles

1 hr. 19:45 min.—1 hr. 6 min.	11
1 hr. 5:59 min.—55:00 min.	16½
54:59—44:00 min.	22
43:59—35:45 min.	27½
under 35:45 min.	33

6.0 Miles

1 hr. 27:00 min.—1 hr. 12 min.	12
1 hr. 11:59 min.—60:00 min.	18
59:59—48:00 min.	24
47:59—39:00 min.	30
under 39:00 min.	36

6.5 Miles

1 hr. 34:14 min.—1 hr. 18 min.	13
1 hr. 17:59 min.—1 hr. 5 min.	19½
1 hr. 4:59 min.—52:00 min.	26
51:59—42:15 min.	32½
under 42:15 min.	39

7.0 Miles

1 hr. 41:29 min.—1 hr. 24 min.	14
1 hr. 23:59 min.—1 hr. 10 min.	21
1 hr. 9:59 min.—56:00 min.	28
55:59—45:30 min.	35
under 45:30 min.	42

7.5 Miles

1 hr. 48:44 min.—1 hr. 30 min.	15
1 hr. 29:59 min.—1 hr. 15 min.	22½
1 hr. 14:59 min.—60:00 min.	30
59:59—48:45 min.	37½
under 48:45 min.	45

8.0 Miles

1 hr. 55:59 min.—1 hr. 36 min.	16
1 hr. 35:59 min.—1 hr. 20 min	24
1 hr. 19:59 min.—1 hr. 4 min.	32
1 hr. 3:59 min.—52:00 min.	40
under 52:00 min.	48

8.5 Miles

2 hrs. 3:14 min.—1 hr. 42 min.	17
1 hr. 41:59 min.—1 hr. 25 min.	25½
1 hr. 24:59 min.—1 hr. 8 min.	34
1 hr. 7:59 min.—55:15 min.	42½
under 55:15 min.	51

9.0 Miles

2 hrs. 10:29 min.—1 hr. 48 min.	18
1 hr. 47:59 min.—1 hr. 30 min.	27
1 hr. 29:59 min.—1 hr. 12 min.	36
1 hr. 11:59 min.—58:30 min.	45
under 58:30 min.	54

9.5 Miles

2 hrs. 17:44 min.—1 hr. 54 min.	19
1 hr. 53:59 min.—1 hr. 35 min.	28½
1 hr. 34:59 min.—1 hr. 16 min.	38
1 hr. 15:59 min.—61:45 min.	47½
Under 61:45 min.	57

10.0 Miles

2 hrs. 24:59—2 hrs.	20
1 hr. 59:59 min.—1 hr. 40 min.	30
1 hr. 39:59 min.—1 hr. 20 min.	40
1 hr. 19:59 min.—1 hr. 5 min.	50
under 1 hr. 5:00 min.	60

Appendix: The Point System Expanded

SWIMMING

200 Yards

6:40 min. or longer	0
6:39— 5:00 min.	1
4:59— 3:20 min.	1½
under 3:20 min.	2½

250 Yards

8:20 min. or longer	0
8:19— 6:15 min.	1¼
6:14— 4:10 min.	2
under 4:10 min.	3

300 Yards

10:00 min. or longer	1*
9:59— 7:30 min.	1½
7:29— 5:00 min.	2½
under 5:00 min.	3½

350 Yards

11:40 min. or longer	1*
11:39— 8:45 min.	2
8:44— 5:50 min.	3
under 5:50 min.	4½

400 Yards

13:20 min. or longer	1*
13:19—10:00 min.	2½
9:59— 6:40 min.	3½
under 6:40 min.	5

450 Yards

15:00 min. or longer	1*
14:59—11:15 min.	3
11:14— 7:30 min.	4
under 7:30 min.	5½

500 Yards

16:40 min. or longer	1*
16:39—12:30 min.	3
12:29— 8:20 min.	4
under 8:20 min.	6

550 Yards

18:20 min. or longer	1*
18:19—13:45 min.	3½
13:44— 9:10 min.	4½
under 9:10 min.	7

600 Yards

20:00 min. or longer	1½*
19:59—15:00 min.	4
14:59—10:00 min.	5
under 10:00 min.	7½

650 Yards

21:40 min. or longer	1½*
21:39—16:15 min.	4
16:14—10:50 min.	5½
under 10:50 min.	8

700 Yards

23:20 min. or longer	1½
23:19—17:30 min.	4½
17:29—11:40 min.	6
under 11:40 min.	8½

750 Yards

25:00 min. or longer	1½*
24:59—18:45 min.	4¾
18:44—12:30 min.	6½
under 12:30 min.	9½

800 Yards

26:40 min. or longer	1½
26:39—20:00 min.	5
19:59—13:20 min.	6½
under 13:20 min.	10

850 Yards

28:20 min. or longer	1½*
28:19—21:15 min.	5¼
21:14—14:10 min.	7
under 14:10 min.	10½

900 Yards

30:00 min. or longer	2*
29:59—22:30 min.	5½
22:29—15:00 min.	7½
under 15:00 min.	11¼

950 Yards

31:40 min. or longer	2*
31:39—23:15 min.	5¾
23:14—15:50 min.	8
under 15:50 min.	12

1000 Yards

33:20 min. or longer	2*
33:19—25:00 min.	6¼
24:59—16:40 min.	8½
under 16:40 min.	12½

1100 Yards

36:40 min. or longer	2*
36:39—27:30 min.	7
27:29—18:20 min.	9
under 18:20 min.	13¾

1200 Yards

40:00 min. or longer	2½*
39:59—30:00 min.	7½
29:59—20:00 min.	10
under 20:00 min.	15

1300 Yards

43:20 min. or longer	2½*
43:19—32:30 min.	8
32:29—21:40 min.	11
under 21:40 min.	16¼

1400 Yards

46:40 min. or longer	2½*
46:39—35:00 min.	8¾
34:59—23:20 min.	11½
under 23:20 min.	17½

1500 Yards

50:00 min. or longer	3*
49:59—37:30 min.	9½
37:29—25:00 min.	12½
under 25:00 min.	18¾

1600 Yards

53:20 min. or longer	3*
53:19—40:00 min.	10
39:59—26:40 min.	13¼
under 26:40 min.	20

1700 Yards

56:40 min. or longer	3*
56:39—42:30 min.	10½
42:29—28:20 min.	14
under 28:20 min.	21¼

1800 Yards

1 hr. or longer	3½*
59:59—45:00 min.	11
44:59—30:00 min.	15
under 30:00 min.	22½

1900 Yards

1 hr. 3:20 min. or longer	3½*
1 hr. 3:19—47:30 min.	12
47:29—31:40 min.	15¾
under 31:40 min.	23¾

2000 Yards

1 hr. 6:40 min. or longer	3½*
1 hr. 6:39—50:00 min.	12½
49:59—33:20 min.	16½
under 33:20 min.	25

*Exercise of sufficient duration to be of cardiovascular benefit. At this speed, ordinarily no training effect would occur. However, the duration is of such extent that a training effect does begin to occur.

ADDITIONAL COMMENTS:

Points calculated on overhand crawl, i.e., 9.0 Kcal per min. Breaststroke is less demanding: 7.0 Kcal per min. Backstroke, a little more: 8.0 Kcal per min. Butterfly, most demanding: 12.0 Kcal per min.

Appendix: The Point System Expanded

CYCLING

INSTRUCTIONS:

1. Points determined considering equal uphill and downhill course.
2. Points determined considering equal time with and against the wind.
3. For cycling a one way course constantly against a wind exceeding 5 MPH, add ½ point per mile to the total point value.

2.0 Miles			7.0 Miles	
12 min. or longer	0		42 min. or longer	1½*
11:59— 8:00 min.	1		41:59—28:00 min.	3½
7:59— 6:00 min.	2		27:59—21:00 min.	7
under 6:00 min.	3		under 21:00 min.	10½

3.0 Miles			8.0 Miles	
18 min. or longer	0		48 min. or longer	1½*
17:59—12:00 min.	1½		47:59—32:00 min.	4
11:59— 9:00 min.	3		31:59—24:00 min.	8
under 9:00 min.	4½		under 24:00 min.	12

4.0 Miles			9.0 Miles	
24 min. or longer	0		54:00 min. or longer	2*
23:59—16:00 min.	2		53:59—36:00 min.	4½
15:59—12:00 min.	4		35:59—27:00 min.	9
under 12:00 min.	6		under 27:00 min.	13½

5.0 Miles			10.0 Miles	
30 min. or longer	1*		1 hr. or longer	2*
29:59—20:00 min.	2½		59:59—40:00 min.	5
19:59—15:00 min.	5		39:59—30:00 min.	10
under 15:00 min.	7½		under 30:00 min.	15

6.0 Miles			11.0 Miles	
36 min. or longer	1*		1 hr. 6:00 min. or longer	2½*
35:59—24:00 min.	3		1 hr. 5:59 min.—44:00 min.	5½
23:59—18:00 min.	6		43:59—33:00 min.	11
under 18:00 min.	9		under 33:00 min.	16½

12.0 Miles

1 hr. 12:00 min. or longer	2½*
1 hr. 11:59 min.—48:00 min.	6
47:59—36:00 min.	12
under 36:00 min.	18

13.0 Miles

1 hr. 18 min. or longer	3*
1 hr. 17:59 min.—52:00 min.	6½
51:59—39:00 min.	13
under 39:00 min.	19½

14.0 Miles

1 hr. 24 min. or longer	3*
1 hr. 23:59 min.—56:00 min.	7
55:59—42:00 min.	14
under 42:00 min.	21

15.0 Miles

1 hr. 30 min. or longer	3½*
1 hr. 29:59 min.—1 hr.	7½
59:59—45:00 min.	15
under 45:00 min.	22½

16.0 Miles

1 hr. 36 min. or longer	3½*
1 hr. 35:59 min.—1 hr. 4:00 min.	8
1 hr. 3:59 min.—48:00 min.	16
under 48:00 min.	24

17.0 Miles

1 hr. 42:00 min. or longer	4*
1 hr. 41:59 min.—1 hr. 8 min.	8½]
1 hr. 7:59 min.—51:00 min.	17
under 51:00 min.	25½

18.0 Miles

1 hr. 48:00 min. or longer	4*
1 hr. 47:59 min.—1 hr. 12 min.	9
1 hr. 11:59 min.—54:00 min.	18
under 54:00 min.	27

19.0 Miles

1 hr. 54:00 min. or longer	4½*
1 hr. 53:59 min.—1 hr. 16 min.	9½
1 hr. 15:59 min.—57:00 min.	19
under 57:00 min.	28½

20.0 Miles

2 hrs. or longer	4½*
1 hr. 59:59 min.—1 hr. 20 min.	10
1 hr. 19:59 min.—1 hr.	20
under 1 hr.	30

25.0 Miles

2 hrs. 30:00 min. or longer	6*
2 hrs. 29:59 min.—1 hr. 40 min.	12½
1 hr. 39:59 min.—1 hr. 15 min.	25
under 1 hr. 15:00 min.	37½

30.0 Miles

3 hrs. or longer	7*
2 hrs. 59:59 min.—2 hrs.	15
1 hr. 59:59 min.—1 hr. 30 min.	30
under 1 hr. 30:00 min.	45

---

*Exercise of sufficient duration to be of cardiovascular benefit. At this speed, ordinarily no training effect would occur. However, the duration is of such extent that a training effect does begin to occur.

WALKING

1.0 Miles

20:00 min. or longer	0
19:59—14:30 min.	1
14:29—12:00 min.	2

1.5 Miles

30:00 min. or longer	0
29:59—21:45 min.	1½
21:44—18:00 min.	3

2.0 Miles

40:00 min. or longer	1*
39:59—29:00 min.	2
28:59—24:00 min.	4

2.5 Miles

50:00 min. or longer	1*
49:59—36:15 min.	2½
36:14—30:00 min.	5

3.0 Miles

1 hr. or longer	1½*
59:59—43:30 min.	3
43:29—36:00 min.	6

3.5 Miles

1 hr. 10:00 min. or longer	1½*
1 hr. 9:59 min.—50:45 min.	3½
50:44—42:00 min.	7

4.0 Miles

1 hr. 20:00 min. or longer	2*
1 hr. 19:59 min.—58:00 min.	4
57:59—48:00 min.	8

4.5 Miles

1 hr. 30:00 min. or longer	2*
1 hr. 29:59 min.—1 hr. 5:15 min.	4½
1 hr. 5:14 min.—54:00 min.	9

5.0 Miles

1 hr. 40:00 min. or longer	2½*
1 hr. 39:59 min.—1 hr. 12:30 min.	5
1 hr. 12:29 min.—1 hr.	10

5.5 Miles

1 hr. 50:00 min. or longer	2½*
1 hr. 49:59 min.—1 hr. 19:45 min.	5½
1 hr. 19:44 min.—1 hr. 6:00 min.	11

6.0 Miles

2 hrs. or longer	3*
1 hr. 59:59 min.—1 hr. 27:00 min.	6
1 hr. 26:59 min.—1 hr. 12:00 min.	12

6.5 Miles

2 hrs. 10:00 min. or longer	3*
2 hrs. 9:59 min.—1 hr. 34:15 min.	6½
1 hr. 34:14 min.—1 hr. 18:00 min.	13

7.0 Miles

2 hrs. 20:00 min. or longer	3½*
2 hrs. 19:59 min.—1 hr. 41:30 min.	7
1 hr. 41:29 min.—1 hr. 24:00 min.	14

7.5 Miles

2 hrs. 30:00 min. or longer	3½*
2 hrs. 29:59 min.—1 hr. 48:45 min.	7½
1 hr. 48:44 min.—1 hr. 30:00 min.	15

8.0 Miles

2 hrs. 40:00 min. or longer   **4***
2 hrs. 39:59 min.—1 hr. 56:00 min. 8
1 hr. 55:59 min.—1 hr. 36:00 min. 16

8.5 Miles

2 hrs. 50:00 min. or longer   **4***
2 hrs. 49:59 min.—2 hrs. 3:15 min. 8½
2 hrs. 3:14 min.—1 hr. 42:00 min. 17

9.0 Miles

3 hrs. or longer   **4½***
2 hrs. 59:59 min.—2 hrs. 10:30 min. 9
2 hrs. 10:29 min.—1 hr. 48:00 min. 18

9.5 Miles

3 hrs. 10:00 min. or longer   **4½***
3 hrs. 9:59 min.—2 hrs. 17:45 min. 9½
2 hrs. 17:44 min.—1 hr. 54 min. 19

10.0 Miles

3 hrs. 20:00 min. or longer   **5***
3 hrs. 19:59 min.—2 hrs. 25 min. 10
2 hrs. 24:59 min.—2 hrs. 20

*Exercise of sufficient duration to be of cardiovascular benefit. At this speed, ordinarily no training effect would occur. However, the duration is of such extent that a training effect does begin to occur.

STATIONARY RUNNING

TIME	*60-70 STEPS/MIN	POINTS	*70-80 STEPS/MIN	POINTS	*80-90 STEPS/MIN	POINTS
2:30	150- 175	½	175- 200	¾	200- 225	1
5:00	300- 350	1¼	350- 400	1½	400- 450	2
7:30	450- 525	2	525- 600	2¼	600- 675	3
10:00	600- 700	2½	700- 800	3	800- 900	4
12:30	750- 875	3¼	875-1000	3¾	1000-1125	5
15:00	900-1050	3¾	1050-1200	4½	1200-1350	6
17:30	1050-1225	4¼	1225-1400	5¼	1400-1575	7
20:00	1200-1400	5	1400-1600	6	1600-1800	8
22:30	1350-1575	5½	1575-1800	6¾	1800-2025	9
25:00	1500-1750	6¼	1750-2000	7½	2000-2250	10

*Count only when the left foot hits the floor. Feet must be brought at least 8 inches from the floor.

Appendix: The Point System Expanded

HANDBALL/SQUASH/BASKETBALL*

DURATION	POINTS	DURATION	POINTS
10 min.	1½	55 min.	8¼
15 min.	2¼	60 min.	9
20 min.	3	65 min.	9¾
25 min.	3¾	70 min.	10½
30 min.	4½	75 min.	11¼
35 min.	5¼	80 min.	12
40 min.	6	85 min.	12¾
45 min.	6¾	90 min.	13½
50 min.	7½		

*Continuous exercise. Do not include breaks, etc.

ADDITIONAL EXERCISES

		POINTS*			POINTS*
Fencing	10 min.	1	Skating	15 min.	1
	20 min.	2	(ice or roller)	30 min.	2
	30 min.	3		60 min.	4
Football**	30 min.	3	Skiing***	30 min.	3
	60 min.	6	(snow or water)	60 min.	6
	90 min.	9		90 min.	9
Golf	9 holes	1½	Soccer and Lacrosse**	30 min.	3
(No motorized carts!)	18 holes	3		60 min.	6
				90 min.	9
Hockey	20 min.	3			
	40 min.	6	Tennis	1 set	1½
	60 min.	9	(singles only)	2 sets	3
	80 min.	12		3 sets	4½
Rope Skipping	5 min.	1½	Volleyball	15 min.	1
(continuous)	10 min.	3		30 min.	2
	15 min.	4½		60 min.	4
Rowing	6 min.	1	Wrestling	5 min.	2
(2 oars, 20 strokes/	18 min.	3		10 min.	4
min.)	36 min.	6		15 min.	6

*Points based on caloric requirements expressed in the scientific literature.
**Count only the time in which you are actively participating.
***Count only the time in which you are actively skiing.

Bibliographic Notes

CHAPTER

1 (No references)

2 Åstrand, P. O. "Human Physical Fitness with Special Reference to Sex and Age," *Physiological Reviews,* Vol. 36, No. 3, July 1956.

Katz, L. N. "Physical Fitness and Coronary Heart Disease," *Circulation,* Vol. 35, February 1967, p405.

Knehr, C. A., D. B. Dill, and William Neufeld. "Training and Its Effects on Man at Rest and at Work," *American Journ. of Physiology,* Vol. 136, No. 1, March 1942.

3 Higdon, Hal. "Let's Tell the Truth About Isometrics," *Today's Health,* June 1965.

Alley, Louis. Problems of Sports Medicine Encountered in a Large University, Physical Education Department. Presented at the 12th Annual Meeting of the American College of Sports Medicine, Dallas, Texas, March 1965.

Roskamm, H. "Optimum Patterns of Exercise for Healthy Adults," *Canad. Med. Ass. Journ.,* March 25, 1967, Vol. 96, pp895-899.

Massey, B. H., R. C. Nelson, B. C. Sharkey, and T. Comden. "Effect of High Frequency Electrical Stimulation on the Size and Strength of Skeletal Muscle," *Journ. Sports Med.,* Vol. 5, No. 3, September 1965, pp136-144.

4 Consolazio, C. F., R. E. Johnson, and L. J. Pecora. *Physiological Measurements of Metabolic Functions in Man,* Mc-Graw-Hill Book Company, 1963.

Glassford, R. G., G. H. Y. Baycroft, A. W. Sedgwick, and R. B. J. MacNab. "Comparison of Maximal Oxygen Uptake Values Determined by Predicted and Actual Methods," *Journ. Appl. Physiol.,* Vol. 20, No. 3, May 1965.

Newton, J. L. "The Assessment of Maximal Oxygen Intake," *Journ. Sports Med.*, 3, June-September 1963, pp164-169.

Johnson, R. E., L. Brouha, and R. C. Darling. "A Test of Physical Fitness for Strenuous Exertion," *Revue Canadienne de Biologie,* Vol. 1, No. 5, June 1942.

Taylor, H. L., E. Buskirk, and A. Henschel. "Maximal Oxygen Intake as an Objective Measure of the Cardiorespiratory Performance," *Journ. Appl. Physiol.*, 8, 1955, pp73-80.

Mitchell, J. M., Sproule, and C. B. Chapman. "The Physiological Meaning of the Maximal Oxygen Intake Test," *Journ. of Clin. Invest.*, 37, 1958, p538.

Rasch, P. J., and I. D. Wilson. "Correlation of Selected Laboratory Tests of Physical Fitness with Military Endurance," *Military Medicine,* Vol. 129, No. 3, March 1964, pp256-258.

Balke, B. *A Simple Field Test for the Assessment of Physical Fitness,* CARI Report 63-6, Oklahoma City, Okla., Civil Aeromedical Research Institute, Federal Aviation Agency, April 1963.

Cooper, K. H. "Correlation Between Field and Treadmill Testing as a Means of Assessing Maximal Oxygen Intake," Submitted to *Journ. Amer. Med. Ass.* for publication.

Bigbee, R. A., and L. Doolittle. Luther Burbank Junior High School, Burbank, Calif. (Personal Communication).

5 *Today's Health Guide,* by the Amer. Med. Ass., June 1965.

Åstrand, P. O. "Concluding Remarks: Physical Activity and Cardiovascular Health," *Canad. Med. Ass. Journ.,* Vol. 96, March 25, 1967, pp907-911.

6 Rook, A. "An Investigation into the Longevity of Cambridge Sportsmen," *Brit. Med. Journ.,* 8, 1954, p73.

Karvonen, M. J. "Effects of Vigorous Exercise on the Heart," In: *Work and the Heart,* edited by Rosenbaum, F. F., and E. L. Belknap, New York, 1959, Paul B. Hoeber.

Reindell, H., K. Musshoff, and H. Klepzig. "Das Sportherz," *Handbuch der Inneren Medizin,* Vol. 9, Berlin, 1960, Springer.

Naval Aviation News (Grandpaw Pettibone), July 1966.

Cooper, K. H. "Flying Status Insurance," *Aerospace Safety,* 22, March 1966, pp8-10.

Bartlett, F. C. *Fatigue in the Air Pilot,* Rept. 488, Great Britain, Air Ministry, Flying Personnel Research Committee, August 1942.

Davis, D. R. *Pilot Error. Some Laboratory Experiments,* Air Ministry Publication 3139A, London, His Majesty's Stationery Office, 1948.

Cooper, K. H., and S. Leverett. "Physical Conditioning Versus +GZ Tolerance," *Aerospace Medicine,* Vol. 37, May 1966, pp462-465.

Wessel, J. A. An Investigation of the Relation between Man's Fitness for Strenuous Work and His Ability to Withstand High Headward Acceleration, A Dissertation to the Dept. of

Physical Education, The Univ. of Southern Calif., June 1950.

A Study of the Biomedical Problems Related to the Requirements of Troops at Terrestrial Altitudes of 10,000 Feet or Above. Report of the Federation of American Societies for Experimental Biology in Accordance with the Provisions of US Army Contract No. DA-49-092-ARO-9, October 15, 1963.

Stickney, J. C., and E. J. Van Liere. "Acclimatization to Low Oxygen Tension," *Physiological Reviews*, No. 33, January 1953, pp13-30.

Degner, E. A., K. G. Ikels, and T. H. Allen. "Dissolved Nitrogen and Bends in Oxygen-Nitrogen Mixtures during Exercise at Decreased Pressure," *Aerospace Medicine*, Vol. 36, No. 5, May 1965.

Cooper, K. H., E. Dong, B. M. Beller, and J. W. Ord. "A Study Designed to Determine the Effectiveness of Vigorous Exercise in Preventing Bedrest Deconditioning," *Aerospace Medicine*, Vol. 37, No. 3, March 1966. Presented at the 37th Annual Meeting of the Aerospace Medical Ass.

Berry, C. A. "Space Medicine in Perspective—A Critical Review of the Manned Space Program," *Journ. Amer. Med. Ass.* Vol. 201, No. 4, July 24, 1967.

Grimby, G., N. J. Nilsson, and B. Saltin. "Cardiac Output during Submaximal and Maximal Exercise in Active Middle-Aged Athletes," *Journ. of Appl. Physiol.*, Vol. 21, No. 4, July 1966.

Hellerstein, H. K. A Primary and Secondary Coronary Prevention Program—In-Progress Report, Presented at the First International Conference on Preventive Cardiology, Aug. 28, 1964, Burlington, Vt.

Hellerstein, H. K., and A. B. Ford. "Rehabilitation of the Cardiac Patient," *Journ. Amer. Med. Ass.*, Vol. 164, No. 3, May 18, 1957, pp225-231.

Harris, W. E., W. Bowerman, B. McFadden, and T. A. Kerns. "Jogging—An Adult Exercise Program," *Journ. Amer. Med. Ass.*, Vol. 201, No. 10, September 4, 1967.

7 Hellerstein, H. K., T. R. Hornsten, A. N. Goldbarg, A. G. Burlando, E. H. Friedman, E. Z. Hirsh, and S. Marik. "The Influence of Active Conditioning upon Subjects with Coronary Artery Disease: A Progress Report," *Canad. Med. Ass. Journ.*, Vol. 96, March 25, 1967, pp901-903.

8 Knehr, C. A., D. B. Dill, and William Neufeld. "Training and Its Effects on Man at Rest and at Work," *Amer. Journ. of Physiology*, Vol. 136, No. 1, March 1942.

Leon, A. S., and C. M. Bloor. "Effects of Exercise and Its Cessation on Cardiac Blood Supply," *Clinical Research*, Vol. XV, No. 2, April 1967, p212.

Petren, T., T. Sjostrand, and B. Sylven. "The Influence of Conditioning Training on the Capillaries in the Heart and Skeletal Muscles," *Arbeitsphysiol.*, 9, 1936, pp376-386.

Costill, D. L. "The Relationship between Selected Physiological Variables and Distance Running Performance," *Journ. Sports Med. and Phys. Fitness*, 7, June 1967, pp61-66.

Stevenson, J. A. F., V. Feleki, P. Rechnitzer, and J. R. Beaton. "Effect of Exercise on Coronary Tree Size in the Rat," *Circulation Research*, Vol. XV, September 1964, pp265-269.

Zoll, P. M., S. Wessler, and J. J. Schlesinger. "Interarterial Coronary Anastomoses in the Human Heart, with Particular Reference to Anemia and Relative Cardiac Anoxia," *Circulation*, Vol. IV, No. 6, December 1951, pp797-815.

Skinner, J. S., J. O. Holloszy, and T. K. Cureton. "Effects of a Program of Endurance Exercises on Physical Work," *Amer. Journ. Cardiol.*, 14, December 1964, p747.

Frick, M. H., A. Konettinen, and H. S. Sarajas. "Effects of Physical Training on Circulation at Rest and during Exercise," *Amer. Journ. Cardiol.*, 14, 1963, p142.

Bakle, B. *Experimental Evaluation of Work Capacity as Related to Chronological and Physiological Ageing*, Civil Aeromedical Research Institute, FAA Okla. City, Okla., CARI Report, September 1963, 63-18.

Raab, W., P. DePaula E. Silva, H. Marchet, E. Kimura, and Y. K. Starcheska. "Cardiac Adrenergic Preponderance Due to Lack of Physical Exercise and Its Pathogenic Implications," *Amer. Journ. Cardiol.*, 5, 1960, p300.

Guild, W. R. "Echoes of the Marathon," *New England Journ. of Medicine*, 257, December 12, 1957, pp1165-1170.

Trulson, M. F., R. E. Clancy, W. J. E. Jessop, R. W. Childers, and F. J. Stare. "Comparison of Siblings in Boston and Ireland," *Journ. of the Amer. Dietetic Ass.*, Vol. 45, 1964.

Mann, G. V., R. D. Shaffer, R. S. Anderson, et al. "Cardiovascular Disease in the Masai," *Journ. Atherosclerosis Res.*, 4, July-August 1964, pp289-312.

Gsell, D., and J. Mayer. "Low Blood Cholesterol Associated with High Calorie, High Saturated Fat Intakes in a Swiss Alpine Village Population," *The American Journ. of Clinical Nutrition*, Vol. 10, No. 6, June 1962, pp471-479.

Holloszy, J. O., J. S. Skinner, G. Toro, and T. K. Cureton. "Effects of a Six Month Program of Endurance Exercise on the Serum Lipids of Middle-Aged Men," *Amer. Journ. of Cardiol.*, Vol. 14, December 1964, pp753-760.

Naughton, J., and J. F. McCoy. "Observations on the Relationship of Physical Activity to the Serum Cholesterol Concentration of Healthy Men and Cardiac Patients," *Journ. Chronic Diseases*, Vol. 19, 1966, pp727-733.

"Exercise and Fitness." Special Report by a joint committee of the American Medical Association and the American Association for Health, Physical Education and Recreation, *Journ. Amer. Med. Ass.*, Vol. 188, No. 5, May 4, 1964.

Roskamm, H. "Optimum Patterns of Exercise for Healthy Adults," *Canad. Med. Ass. Journ.*, Vol. 96, No. 12, March 25, 1967, pp895-899.

Roberts, J. T., J. T. Wearn, and J. J. Badal. "The Capillary-Muscle Ratio in Normal & Hypertrophied Human Hearts," *Proc. for Soc. Exp. Biol. & Med.*, Vol. 38, 1938, pp322-323.

Currens, J. H., and P. D. White. "Half a Century of Running," *New England Journ. of Med.*, Vol. 265, No. 20, November 1961, pp988-993.

Faulkner, J. A. "Effect of Cardiac Conditioning on the Anticipatory, Exercise, and Recovery Heart Rates of Young Men, *Journ. of Sports Medicine and Physical Fitness*, Vol. 4, No. 2, June 1964, pp79-86.

Appleton, L., and F. J. Kobes. West Point Studies Concerning the Predictive Value of Initial Physical Performance Levels of Freshmen, Presented at the 12th Annual Meeting of the American College of Sports Medicine, March 17, 1965, Dallas, Texas.

Hammett, V. B. O. "Psychological Changes with Physical Fitness Training," *Canad. Med. Ass. Journ.*, Vol. 96, March 25, 1967, pp764-769.

Cassin, S., R. D. Gilbert, and E. M. Johnson. *Capillary Development During Exposure to Chronic Hypoxia*, USAF School of Aerospace Medicine Technical Documentary Report 66-16, Brooks AFB, Texas.

Cooper, K. H. "Heart Disease and Flying Status: Report of a Case," *Aerospace Medicine*, Vol. 38, No. 9, September 1967, pp964-967.

Chapman, C. B. "Exercise and Heart Disease," *International Forum*, Parke Davis & Co., Therapeutic Notes, Vol. 15, No. 1, January 1967, pp16-18.

Asthma and Activity, Discussed in: *U.S. Medicine*, September 15, 1966.

Wier, J. A., J. M. Schless, L. E. O'Commor, and O. L. Weiser. "Ambulatory Treatment of Tuberculosis: Results in 105 Tuberculous Patients Treated with Chemotherapy and Active Physical Rehabilitation," *American Review of Respiratory Disease*, 84, 1961, pp17-22.

Hirsch, J. G., Schaedler, and Pierce. "A Study Comparing the Effects of Bed Rest and Physical Activity on Recovery from Pulmonary Tuberculosis," *Amer. Rev. Tuberculosis*, No. 75, 1957, p359.

Gertler, M. M. "Ischemic Heart Disease, Heredity and Body Build as Affected by Exercise," *Canad. Med. Ass. Journ.*, Vol. 96, March 25, 1967, pp728-730.

Rosenman, R. H., M. Friedman, R. Strauss, M. Wurm, R. Kositchek, W. Hahn, and N. T. Werthessen. "A Predictive Study of Coronary Heart Disease," *Journ. Amer. Med. Ass.*, Vol. 189, No. 1, July 6, 1964.

Hellerstein, H. K., T. R. Hornsten, A. Goldbarg, A. G. Burlando, E. H. Friedman, E. Z. Hirsch, and S. Marik. "The Influence of Active Conditioning upon Subjects with Coronary Artery Disease: Cardiorespiratory Changes during Training in 67 Patients," *Canad. Med. Ass. Journ.*, Vol. 96, March 25, 1967, pp758-759.

Barry, A. J. "Physical Activity and Psychic Stress/Strain," *Canad. Med. Ass. Journ.,* Vol. 96, March 25, 1967, pp848-851.

Kraus, H., and W. Raab. *Hypokinetic Disease-Diseases Produced by Lack of Exercise,* Charles C. Thomas, Springfield, Ill., 1961.

Raab, W. "Key Position of Catecholamines in Functional and Degenerative Cardiovascular Pathology," *Am. Journ. Cardiol.,* 5, 1960, p571.

Raab, W. "Preventive Medical Mass Reconditioning Abroad—Why Not in the USA?" *Ann. Int. Med.,* 54, 1961, p1191.

Kennedy, J. F. "The Soft American," *Sports Illustrated,* December 26, 1960.

Morris, J. N., and J. A. Heady. "Mortality in Relation to the Physical Activity of Work," *British Journ. of Int. Med.,* 10, 1953, pp245-254.

Morris, J. N., and M. D. Crawford. "Coronary Heart Disease and Physical Activity of Work; Evidence of a National Necropsy Survey," *Brit. Med. Journ.,* 2, 1958, p1485.

Russek, H. I. "Emotional Stress and the Etiology of Coronary Artery Disease," *Am. Journ. Cardiology,* 2, 1958, p129.

McPherson, B. D., A. Paivio, M. S. Yuhaz, P. A. Rechnitzer, H. A. Pickard, and N. M. Lefcoe. "Psychological Effects of an Exercise Program for Post Infarct and Normal Adult Men," *Journ. Sports Med. and Physical Fitness,* 7, June 1967, pp61-66.

Selye, Hans. The Role of Stress in the Production and Prevention of Experimental Cardiopathies. Presented at the First International Conference on Preventive Cardiology, August 1964.

Raab, W. "Metabolic Protection and Reconditioning of the Heart Muscle through Habitual Physical Exercise," *Ann. Int. Med.,* 53, 1960, p87.

Doyle, J. T., T. R. Dawber, W. B. Kannel, S. H. Kinch, and M. A. Kahn. "The Relationship of Cigarette Smoking to Coronary Heart Disease—The Second Report of the Combined Experience of the Albany, N. Y., and Framingham, Mass., Studies," *Journ. Amer. Med. Ass.,* Vol. 190, December 7, 1964, pp886-890.

Smoking and Health, The Report of the Surgeon General's Advisory Committee, 1964.

Morris, J. N., J. A. Heady, P. A. B. Raffle, C. G. Robert, and J. W. Parks. "Coronary Heart Disease and Physical Activity of Work," *The Lancet,* 2, 1953, p1053 and p1111.

Hammond, E. C., and D. Horn. "The Relationship between Human Smoking Habits and Death Rates," *Journ. Am. Med. Ass.,* 155, 1954, p1316.

Taylor, H. L. "The Occupational Factors in the Study of Coronary Heart Disease and Physical Activity," *Canad. Med. Ass. Journ.,* Vol. 96, March 25, 1967, pp825-831.

Frank, C. W., E. Weinblatt, S. Shapiro, and R. V. Sager. "Physical Inactivity as a Lethal Factor in Myocardial Infarction among Men," *Circulation*, Vol. 34, December 1966, pp1022-1033.

Fox, S. M., and J. S. Skinner. "Physical Activity and Cardiovascular Health," *Amer. Journ. Cardiol.*, Vol. 14, No. 6, December 1964, pp731-746.

Eckstein, R. W. "Effect of Exercise and Coronary Artery Narrowing on Coronary Collateral Circulation," *Circulation Research*, Vol. V, May 1957, pp230-235.

McAlpin, R. N., and A. A. Kattus. "Adaptation to Exercise in Angina Pectoris," *Circulation*, Vol. 33, February 1966, pp233-269.

Kaufman, J. M., and R. D. Anslow. "Treatment of Refractory Angina Pectoris with Nitroglycerin and Graded Exercise," *Journ. Amer. Med. Ass.*, Vol. 196, No. 2, April 11, 1966, pp137-141.

Kattus, A. A. Exercise Conditioning of Cardiovascular System —Effects on Cardiac Patients. Presentation given June 25, 1966, at the American Heart Association Meeting "Exercise and the Heart," Seattle, Wash.

Smith, J. E., and G. J. Kidera. "Treatment of Angina Pectoris with Exercise Stress," *Aerospace Medicine*, Vol. 38, No. 7, July 1967, pp742-745.

Pomeroy, W. C., and P. D. White. "Coronary Heart Disease in Former Football Players," *Journ. Amer. Med. Ass.*, Vol. 167(8), June 7, 1958, pp711-714.

Perera, G. A. "Antihypertensive Drugs versus Symptomatic Treatment in Primary Hypertension-Effect on Survival," *Journ. Amer. Med. Ass.*, 173, 1960, pp11-13.

Mastropaolo, J. A. Exercise Conditioning of Cardiovascular System—Active Intervention in Chicago, Presentation given June 25, 1966, at the American Heart Association Meeting "Exercise and the Heart," Seattle, Wash.

Rosenau & Maxcy. (Effect of Exercise on the Digestive Tract) *Preventive Medicine and Public Health*, 8th Edition, p1118.

Bergstrom, J., and E. Hultman. "Muscle Glycogen Synthesis after Exercise: An Enhancing Factor Localized to the Muscle Cells in Man," *Nature*, Vol. 210, April 16, 1966, pp309-310.

Rowell, L. B., J. R. Blackman, and R. A. Bruce. "Indocyamine Green Clearance and Estimated Hepatic Blood Flow during Mild to Maximal Exercise in Upright Man," *Journ. of Clinical Investigation*, Vol. 43, No. 8, 1964, pp1677-1690.

Cooper, K. H., P. Lempert, and J. F. Culver. "Effect of Exercise on Intraocular Tension and Its Relationship to Open Angle Glaucoma," *Aerospace Medicine*, Vol. 36, No. 1, January 1965.

Adler, F. H. *Physiology of the Eye*, ed. 3, St. Louis, C. V. Mosby Co., 1959, p138.

9 Ageyevets, V. U. "Physical Culture Mass Activity at Industrial Plant Shops as a Means of Improving the Health of Workers

and Raising Technico-Economic Indexes," Moscow, *Teoriya Praktika Fizicheskoy Kul'tury*, No. 10, October 1964, pp47-49.

Raab, W., and L. B. Gilman. "Insurance-Sponsored Preventive, Cardiac Reconditioning Centers in West Germany," *The American Journ. of Cardiology*, Vol. 13, No. 5, May 1964, pp670-673.

Wyndham, C. H. "A Survey of the Causal Factors in Heat Stroke and of Their Prevention in the Gold Mining Industry," *Journ. of the South African Institute of Mining and Metallurgy*, February-May 1966, pp245-258 and 536-540.

Strydom, N. E. et al. "Acclimatization to Humid Heat and the Role of Physical Conditioning," *Journ. of Applied Physiology*, Vol. 21, No. 2, March 1966, pp636-642.

Cooper, K. H., G. O. Gey, and R. Bottenberg. The Effect of Cigarette Smoking on Endurance Performance, Submitted to *Journ. Amer. Med. Ass.* for publication.

10 Kennedy, J. F. "The Soft American," *Sports Illustrated*, December 26, 1960.

Kraus, H., and R. P. Hirschland. "Minimum Muscular Fitness Tests in School Children," *The Research Quarterly*, 25, May 1954, p2.

Beckmann, P. The Combined Environmental-Emotional and Physical Cardiac Reconditioning Program at Ohlstadt, Presented at the First International Conference on Preventive Cardiology, Burlington, Vt., August 24-28, 1964.